THE IMAGE OF ARABS IN MODERN PERSIAN LITERATURE

D1528913

Joya Blondel Saad

University Press of America, Inc.
Lanham • New York • London

Copyright © 1996 by
University Press of America,® Inc.
4720 Boston Way
Lanham, Maryland 20706

3 Henrietta Street
London, WC2E 8LU England

Library of Congress Cataloging-in-Publication Data

Saad, Joya Blondel.
The image of Arabs in modern Persian literature / Joya Blondel Saad.
p.   cm.
Includes bibliographical references.
1. Persian literature--20th century--History and criticism. 2. Arabs in
literature.   I. Title.
PK6412.A7S2   1996   891'.550935203927--dc20   96-5955
CIP

ISBN 0-7618-0329-7 (cloth: alk. ppr.)
ISBN 0-7618-0330-0 (pbk: alk. ppr.)

⊖™The paper used in this publication meets the minimum
requirements of American National Standard for information
Sciences—Permanence of Paper for Printed Library Materials,
ANSI Z39.48—1984

for Amin, Haila and Rashid

Contents

Acknowledgements

I would like to thank Michael C. Hillmann, M. R. Ghanoonparvar, Elizabeth W. Fernea and Gail Minault. Thanks also to Abazar Sepehri, and special thanks to Naji.

Grateful acknowledgment is made to the following for permission to reprint previously published material:

Leonardo P. Alishan: Excerpts from "Trends in Modernist Persian Poetry" by Leonardo P. Alishan, 1982. Ph.D. dissertation, The University of Texas at Austin. Reprinted by permission.

The Calder Educational Trust, London, and John Calder Publishers Ltd.: Excerpts from *The Blind Owl* by Sadegh Hedayat, translated by D. P. Costello, 1969. Published by Grove/Atlantic, Inc., 841 Broadway 4th Floor, New York, NY, 10003. Reprinted by permission.

Center for Iranian Studies, Columbia University: Excerpts from *Plagued by the West* by Jalal Al-e Ahmad, translated by Paul Sprachman, 1982. Published by Caravan Books, Delmar, NY, 12054. Reprinted by permission.

Center for Middle Eastern Studies, The University of Texas at Austin: Excerpts from *Haji Agha* by Sadeq Hedayat, translated by G. M. Wickens, 1979. Center for Middle Eastern Studies, The University of Texas at Austin, Austin, TX, 78712. Reprinted by permission.

Chicago Review: Excerpts from "The Mongol's Shadow" by Sadeq Hedayat, translated by D. A. Shojai, 1969. Reprinted by permission of *Chicago Review*.

M. R. Ghanoonparvar: Excerpts from *The Patient Stone* by Sadeq Chubak, translated with annotations and introduction by M. R. Ghanoonparvar, 1989. Published by Mazda Publishers, PO Box 2603, Costa Mesa, CA, 92626. Reprinted by permission.

John Green: Excerpts from *Lost in the Crowd* by Jalal Al-e Ahmad, translated by John Green, 1985. Three Continents Press, PO Box 38009, Colorado Springs, CO, 80937. Reprinted by permission of Three Continents.

Michael C. Hillmann: Excerpts from *A Lonely Woman: Forugh Farrokhzad and Her Poetry* by Michael C. Hillmann, 1987. Three Continents Press, PO Box 38009, Colorado Springs, CO, 80937, and Mage Publishers Inc., 1032 29th St. NW, Washington, DC, 20007. Reprinted by permission of Three Continents and Mage.

Chapter 1

Introduction

This work examines the image of Arabs in modern Persian literature, as part of the issue of defining an Iranian Self in terms of an Arab Other. This work offers a reading of literary texts, treating the image of Arabs and its significance in a literary and social context.

In dealing with the image of Arabs, this work inescapably deals as well with the image of Islam, associated as it is with Arabs, and its relationship to a definition of Iranianness. The Arab Other, as opposed to the Western Other, was chosen because of historical sensitivity to the Arab invasion of Iran in the 7th century CE and subsequent Islamization of Iran, reflected in the intellectual discourse and modern literature of the 20th century, and because that discourse reflects very different understandings of the Iranian Self in relation first to an Arab and then to a Western Other. Furthermore, these different understandings are directly related to the different nationalisms of the Pahlavi monarchy and the Islamic Republic of Iran.

Chapter 1, the "Introduction," sets the ground with a discussion of the problem of self-definition, and the role of literature in the process. It describes Iran as a multi-ethnic state, outlines 19th and 20th century Iranian nationalism, and discusses Arabs and Iranians.

Chapter 2, "Men's Writings, Men's Views," and Chapter 3, "Women's Writings, Women's Views," establish the issue. Both chapters treat Persian novels, short stories, essays and poems by major Iranian writers of the 20th century in terms of the images they present of Arabs, with an emphasis on the literature of the Pahlavi period (1921-1979). Rather than catalogue all of modern Persian literature, Chapter 2 focuses on works by Mohammad Ali Jamâlzâdeh, Sâdeq Hedâyat, Sâdeq Chubak, Mehdi Akhavân-e Sâles, and Nâder Nâderpour; while Chapter 3 focuses on works by Forugh Farrokhzâd, Tâhereh Saffârzâdeh, and Simin Dâneshvar. The works chosen serve to represent the spectrum of writing and opinion, while the two chapters counterpose the polar ends of that spectrum.

Chapter 4, called "A Man in the Middle," goes on to discuss the works of Jalâl Âl-e Ahmad as a case study, as the fairest and most revealing analysis of a prominent writer, sympathetic both to Persian Iranian cultural nationalism and to Islam.

Chapter 5, "Conclusion," summarizes findings and suggests further avenues of investigation into Iranian identity through the scrutiny of Persian literature.

All Persian words cited are transliterated from the Arabic script using the system recommended by Naser Sharify. (1) A circumflex over /a/ distinguishes the sound /â/ as in "Tehrân" from the sound /a/ as in "Mashhad." In the case of some proper names, popular spelling and writers' personal preferences are used.

The Issue of Self-Definition and the Role of Literature in the Process

Ever since "nation" joined God, king and beloved as objects of poetic address in Persian literature at the beginning of the 20th century, the problem of defining that nation has persisted. This is a literary problem, as well as a social and political problem, and a personal problem, reflected in literature. It is a search for a national cultural and historical identity, and for an authentic self-definition. It is a problem for Persian Iranians obviously, but also for Arab Iranians, other Iranian minorities, such as Âzarbâyjâni Turkish Iranians, and for non-Iranian readers as well.

This work will look at the problem from the point of view of writers of modern Persian Iranian literature as they define Iran as a nation and themselves as Iranian by defining the Arab as the Other, a reverse definition of Iranian as the Self, for some in terms of race or language, for others in terms of religion, history and culture as well. All of this, as such, is part of the creation of an "Iranian" national identity in the 20th century.

Of course the Arab is not the only Other. For modern Persian writers, the Western Other has been of primary importance. As M. R.

Ghanoonparvar points out, "In their attempt to respond to the forces of modernity and external influences, Iranian writers have portrayed Western characters in their work, and the West and Western values and those who espouse them have become recurrent features." (2) Moreover, the Arab Other is a metaphor to be seen on many levels. Criticism of things Arab may represent criticism of things Iranian that would otherwise not be publishable, for example, criticism of the Iranian monarchy or of Islamic institutions. The Arab Other may also represent the Western Other, whose importance grew as the West encroached upon Iran and the region.

The influence of modern Persian literature upon Iranian society at large, some would argue, has been small, even negligible; given the high rate of illiteracy, such literature is not "popular" except among a small group of writers and intellectuals. (3)   On the other hand, according to Manochehr Dorraj,

> in the developing countries, due to the relative economic and political impotence of the ruling elite and the high rate of illiteracy, the intelligentsia plays an especially important role in the political life.... First, because the division of labor is not as refined in the Third World as in the West, intellectuals perform multiple social roles. A playwright might also be a school teacher or a doctor. This diversity of social functions adds to the significance of their already rare skills. Second, due to the closed nature of the political system and prevalence of political repression in most of the Third World countries, intellectuals become the eyes, ears, and voices of the public. Hence, it follows that the weaker the social institutions, especially those conducive to political participation, the more crucial becomes the role of intellectuals, and the Iranian case is no exception. (4)

Such works are then, at the very least, a reflection of concerns and a range of responses to them. More importantly, however, and surprisingly as well, given the oppositional stance of most modern writers toward the government, the views of some writers on some aspects of Iranian nationalism were in harmony with those of the Pahlavi regime. Indeed, modern literature was chosen for this study because of its connection with nationalism; it is the first Iranian literature intended for a broad audience.

According to Michael Hillmann, one would expect to find nationalist sentiment in modern Persian literature for a number of reasons: modernist writers are part of the intelligentsia, intimately acquainted with Western ideas including political nationalism;

modernist literature has been from the beginning consciously realistic and *engagé*; and because from the beginning as well, modernist literature has attempted to speak to the broad masses of the people, not just a literary or courtly elite, and to make the people educated and responsible members of modern society. (5)

Cultural nationalism is a persistent theme in modern Persian literature, implied through the depiction of social history, local color, regional customs, dialects and so on, all of which imply the author's deep attachment to the region. (6) In "Ziyârat" [The Pilgrimage] (1945), Jalâl Âl-e Ahmad, setting out on a pilgrimage to Karbalâ, describes his attachment to the Iran he is leaving:

> I could think of nothing but the soup which would be prepared at home after I had gone—the soup with the long thin noodles which my sister would cut, the bowls full of mint with the marks of burning on them which would be sent to my relatives, and the party and the feast that would be held at home in honor of the occasion, and finally the prayers that would surely be said at the party for my safe return.
> Well, that is Iran. And those are her customs: The vegetable pilaw with fish on New Year's Eve, the New Year's display of seven things that begin with the letter 's', the rice soup, the samanu, the noodle soup, and a thousand other things like them. Customs that at first sight seem silly, useless, trivial; but which in reality are created by and conform to the pattern of that special Iranian life...Oh Iran, Iran! (7)

On the other hand, political nationalism, as opposed to cultural nationalism or social criticism, is seldom a theme, because many authors, like many Iranians, saw Iran as a nation-state defined only by international borders and a central government. (8) A further problem is that the nationalist ideology held by many of these modernist Persian writers, most of whom were anti-establishment, was in fact the same ideology, emphasizing modernization, secularization and Persian Iranian political nationalism, held by the Pahlavi regime. (9)

Nationalism means loyalty and devotion to a nation. The problem is, how does one define a nation? According to Shâhrokh Meskoob, since the coming of Islam to Iran, Iranian national consciousness has been based on the Persian language and pre-Islamic history: "Only with respect to two things were we Iranians separate from other Muslims: history and language, the two factors on which we proceeded to build our own identity as a people or nation." (10) Given that understanding of Iran as a nation defined by a common language and history, it is not surprising that, from the start, modern Persian Iranian literature has been intimately involved in the question of Iranian nationalism, defining Iranianness largely in terms of its own Persian language, history and culture. As Hassan Kamshad points out,

> A major Iranian problem has always been to maintain a distinct and integrated civilization despite a heterogeneous ethnic composition and the frequent inroads of other peoples. Thus a standard literary language has through the centuries assumed vast importance: but for literary Persian, disuniting forces might have proceeded almost without restraint. (11)

Iran as a Multi-ethnic State

There is, however, a problem with Meskoob's definition of an Iranian nation. Iran is a country of great ethnic diversity. Demographically the country may be very roughly divided into two concentric circles, the smaller, inside circle inhabited by Persians, and the larger, outside circle, broken in the north-east, made up of various other ethnic groups, "group[s] of people who see themselves (or are seen by others) as culturally distinct. They share certain culture traits which usually, but not always, include language, religion, heritage and value systems which they consider right for them." (12) Most significant, in terms of Meskoob's argument, is the fact that Persian is the first language of only about half of the Iranian population. There are substantial numbers, as well, of Âzarbâyjâni Turks, Turkomans, Qashqâi Turks and other Turkic speaking nomadic tribes, Kurds, Lurs, Baluch, Arabs, Armenians, and Assyrians.

The largest non-Persian ethnic groups are the Âzarbâyjâni Turks, Turkmans, Baluch, Kurds, Lurs and Arabs. Each group shares a common language and culture which differentiates them, to a greater or lesser degree, from the other peoples of Iran, as well as, in some cases and to some extent, a common land. The members of these groups are conscious of their ethnic differences, and even groups such as the Armenians and Assyrians, which are not concentrated in one area, have resisted assimilation. The political implications are enormous, especially since these ethnic groups are contiguous with the same peoples across the borders of Iran, in some cases holding political power, in states like Turkey, Iraq, and (formerly Soviet) Turkmenistan and Âzarbâyjân.

While Persian is the official language of Iran, and has been the dominant language on the Iranian plateau since the Achaemenid era

(559-330 BCE), only about half the population speaks Persian as their mother tongue. The official representation of Iran during the Pahlavi era was, in reality, a misrepresentation of Iran as a linguistically and culturally homogeneous nation:

> In some remote parts of Azarbaijan, Khuzistan and other frontier areas, the peasants and tribal people speak a Persian dialect mixed with Turkish or Arabic. The Baluchis have their own dialect too. But one is not conscious of these different tongues because the overwhelming majority, i.e., about 95% of the population of Iran, speak one language—the present-day Persian tongue—and write one script—the present-day Persian writing.
> [The culture of Iran] is characteristically one and unlike the cultures of other countries in Asia or Europe, it is not varied or multi-coloured. (13)

However, at the end of the 19th century, less than half the population spoke Persian, and fifteen percent of the Persian speakers spoke nonstandard dialects that were unintelligible to the main group. Twenty five percent of the population spoke Turkic languages. The rest of the population spoke other languages, including Baluchi, Kurdish and Arabic. (14) The Qâjâr government in Tehrân (ruled 1796-1925) had little control over the rest of Iran. Indeed, the provinces of Khuzestân, Gilân and Khorâsân, as well as many of the nomadic tribes, were practically autonomous by 1919. (15)

19th and 20th Century Iranian Nationalism

At the same time, the 19th century saw the beginning of a modern nationalist consciousness and nationalist movement in Iran. The perception of Iran as backward and powerless, when compared to the West, led secular intellectuals of the time to place part of the blame for Iranian backwardness on Islam, and to seek to establish a new and seemingly more authentic definition of Iranianness based on the pre-Islamic past. Fath 'Ali Âkhondzâdeh (1812-1878), Mirzâ Âqâ Khân Kermâni (1853-1896), and many of their contemporaries, portrayed an ancient Achaemenid and Sâsânid Iran whose glorious civilization had been destroyed by 'savage bedouins'. Kermâni saw Islam as an alien religion forced upon the 'noble Aryan nation' by a 'Semitic' nation, 'a handful of naked barefoot lizard-eaters, desert-dwelling nomads, savage Arabs', which had brought about the ruin of Iranian civilization. (16) According to Dorraj, Kermâni "symbolized the profound alienation of the Westernized intellectuals of his generation from the traditional teachings and rituals of Shi'ism when he asked: 'What do I gain—I am an Iranian—from knowing about early Arab Muslim rulers such as Khalid Ibn Walid or Yazid Ibn Mu'awiya? What do I gain from reading all about Ali and his sons?" (17)

According to Mangol Bayat-Philipp, this idealized vision of the pre-Islamic past and the hope to see it resurrected was perhaps the most significant and long-lasting contribution of those intellectuals to the nationalist movement. (18) Indeed, according to Leon Poliakov, the myth of the "Golden Age" is an essential part of nationalism. (19) The modern literature of the pre-constitutional period and up to the beginnings of the Pahlavi regime, mainly newspaper essays, poetry, and historical novels, dealt with government corruption and social backwardness, and spoke out against both the Qâjâr regime and the clergy. (20) Typical of the new literary works were writings attacking the clergy, and glorifying Zoroaster and pre-Islamic Iran. (21)

It should be noted that Kermâni's "savage bedouins" is a common stereotype in Iranian culture, a culture which includes negative images of Arabs which Iranians acquire through education and upbringing. Ferdowsi's *Shâhnâmeh*, the Persian national epic, ends with the coming of the Muslim Arabs, and the overthrow and occupation of Sâsânid Iran. Moreover, those Arabs are portrayed as less prosperous and less civilized than the Iranians. Rostam, leader of the Iranian army, sends a letter to Sa'd, leader of the Arab army, asking in part:

> Over whom do you seek to triumph, you, naked commander of a naked army? With a loaf of bread you are satisfied yet remain hungry. You have neither elephants nor platforms nor baggage nor gear. Mere existence in Iran would be enough for you.... From a diet of camel's milk and lizards the Arabs have come so far as to aspire to the Keyâni throne. Is there no shame in your eyes? (22)

The *Shâhnâmeh* also includes the story of Zahhâk, an Arab, who was deceived by Eblis [the devil] and transformed into a monster with serpents growing out of his shoulders; every night Zahhâk feeds the serpents the brains of two young men. Zahhâk ruled for a thousand years, "an era during which the ways of rational men disappeared and the wishes of the devil-possessed everywhere prevailed. Virtue was humiliated and wizardry esteemed; truth hid itself and evil flourished openly." (23)

But the *Shâhnâmeh* cannot be characterized as wholly anti-Arab. There are positive images as well. Zahhâk's father, Merdâs, king of the

Arabs, is described as "a man who came from the deserts where men rode horses and brandished spears. He was a person much honoured for his generosity and one who in his fear of the Lord trembled as though shaken by a gale." (24) Yazdegerd sends his son Bahrâm to Yemen, to be brought up by Arabs. (25) And, of course, the perennial enemy of Iran in the *Shâhnâmeh* is not the Arabs, but Turân, to the east.

The image of Arabs as poor and uncivilized vis-à-vis Iranians appears again in the 11th century *Safarnâmeh* [Book of Travels] of Nâser Khosrow, a classical literary work. He describes the Arabs he sees on his return from Mecca:

> The entire district of Tâ'ef consists of a wretched little town with a strong fortress. It has a small bazaar and a pitiful little mosque.... From there we proceeded to a district called Thorayyâ.... There is said to be no ruler or sultan in that area: each place has an independent chieftain or headman. The people are robbers and murderers and constantly fight among themselves.... Among one tribe, some seventy-year-old men told me that in their whole lives they had drunk nothing but camels' milk, since in the desert there is nothing but bitter scrub eaten by the camels. They actually imagined that the whole world was like that! ...they were a hungry, naked, and ignorant people. Everyone who came to pray brought his sword and shield with him as a matter of course. (26)

Of course these are not the only Arabs that he meets in the course of his travels; the Arabs of Damascus, Jerusalem, Cairo and Basra live very differently. But the shock of seeing people living in such conditions makes a great impression on him, and presumably on his readers as well.

Clearly, anti-Arab feelings were not imported from the West. But, as Bayat-Philipp points out, 19th century Iranian nationalist thinking was influenced by Western racist theories. (27) This is hardly surprising, since the supposed existence of Aryan and Semitic races "was already a part of the intellectual baggage of all cultivated Europeans" by about 1860, and "by the end of the nineteenth century, international scientific opinion had promoted this division to the status of an axiom." (28) According to Poliakov,

> This pride [of Europeans], indeed, was to increase unchecked as a result of the contrast between the many European [technological] achievements and the inertia which characterized other entire continents. After the end of the seventeenth century those achievements gave rise to the idea of Progress (which perhaps was merely the reverse of the

> Christian idea of the Fall, in the sense that the Golden Age, which occurred before the Fall, was transferred to the future), but the contrast between them and the inertia outside Europe contained the germ of future, highly persuasive racial arguments; because the temptation to attribute a congenital, bio-scientific superiority to white men as the standard-bearers of Progress and the possessors of triumphant Reason became irresistible. (29)

Thus, Westernized Iranian intellectuals not only would have been aware of such theories, given their widespread acceptance and popularity, but would have found in them as well a Western, "scientific" affirmation of their own worth. Since Persians were included among the Aryans, the causes of Iran's backwardness were not "racially" determined, and so there was hope for progress and modernization.

Western racist ideas were indeed known in Iran. Âl-e Ahmad gives an indication of this when he remarks:

> Not only do all of our west-stricken intellectuals back up their opinions with these [orientalist] studies, but I have heard many times that even on the pulpit, in mosques (which are thought to be the last bastion against the West and westitis) where mullahs quote Carlyle, Gustav Le Bon, Gobineau, Edward Browne, and others as final authorities on some personage or event or sect. (30)

The reference is to Comte Arthur de Gobineau, whose *Essai sur l'inégalité des races humaines* (Essay on the Inequality of the Human Races, 1853-55) and *Renaissance* (1877) glorified the "Aryan race" and popularized racist theory. (31)

Western theories of race and nationalism developed hand in hand. The Western national model is a territorial and linguistic/racial construct. It does not allow for a multi-ethnic nationalism because, historically, according to Poliakov, central to nationalism was "the affirmation of a common descent in the rise of national feeling." (32) When science dictated the replacement of Adam as a universal ancestor, scientists and philosophers affiliated European peoples to Eastern ancestors, Indian and Persian. The discovery of the Indo-European family of languages, by William Jones in 1788, seemed to prove that a particular race—a white race—had originated in Asia and spread to Europe. Linguistics named these ancestors the Aryans, and set them in opposition to the Hamites, the Mongols, and the Semites. Linguistic proof became the only scientific proof of the origins of nations, and from the relationship of language was deduced a relationship of race.

(33) Language, as proof of origin, became proof of race. According to Poliakov, "the national characteristics described as pure—whether blood or spirit, origin or stock or people, race or religion—tended to become interchangeable." (34) Indeed, the central motif of racism is "purity," and "miscegenation" the most heinous crime: racial purity is encoded in sexual purity, and miscegenation is a violation of both. It is this same linguistic/racial purity which informs the Western national model and so precludes a multi-ethnic nationalism.

The Western national model was expressed in the ideal of the "fatherland." The unchanging spirit of a people, the *Volkgeist*, was determined by race, refined through history and expressed through language and culture, which was defined in terms of the national language and traditional national literature. The nation was a community separated from others by its own inner spirit, as expressed through its language and culture. (35)

Race refers to heredity, to nature, while ethnicity refers to social and cultural ties, to learning, to nurture. Of course, the concept of race has little utility or validity. Very few human beings could be said to be "racially pure," and most human characteristics are due to cultural, ethnic, differences. (36) But according to this model, "cultural confrontation ... was conceived as a conflict between different bloods," or different races. (37) Clearly, there is a contradiction between Iran's multi-ethnic reality and this Western theory of nationalism. Nevertheless, it was against this background that Rezâ Khân (later Rezâ Shâh Pahlavi) seized power in 1921, and the Western national model became state policy.

Modern Iran is, to a large extent, the result of the policies of Rezâ Shâh, who subdued the autonomous national minorities and nomadic tribes and brought them together to establish Iran as a centralized nation-state. He developed modern armed forces and used them to enforce the control of the central government in Tehrân over the whole country. (38)

Rezâ Shâh militarily conquered Arabestân (Khuzestân), Lurestân, Kurdestân, Baluchestân, Gilân and Mâzandarân, the Turkomans of Khorâsân, and the nomads of Fârs. The government forced nomads to settle in either their summer or winter lands, or in areas far from their own lands, and many animals and people died of starvation, disease and exposure. (39) The army drafted young men from these minority groups, and scattered them to posts throughout the country so that they would form no more than a minority in each unit. New laws required men and women to wear European-style clothing and hats, in place of the distinctive traditional clothing of each ethnic group. (40)

Fundamental to the Pahlavi regime's overall policy to integrate all national minorities into a Persian "Iran" was economic and political centralization in Tehrân, and the destruction of the economic base of non-Persian groups, both the settled minority nations surrounding the Iranian plateau, and the nomadic tribes. Thus, economic development in Iran as a whole was centered in Tehrân. (41)

Rezâ Shâh was responsible for initiating many changes in Iranian society. He limited the political power of the Shi'i Muslim clergy, and forbade the use of the Islamic lunar calendar in business, replacing it with the Iranian solar calendar. Under Rezâ Shâh, development of educational, health, transportation and banking systems was begun. (42)

But Rezâ Shâh did not address such fundamental problems of Iranian society as land reform. Instead, he continued to impose superficial social reforms, many of them extremely unpopular, like the prohibition of the veiling of women. The government dealt with people's discontent by disseminating nationalistic Persian slogans and cultural propaganda recalling the glories of the ancient pre-Islamic Persian empire, which had little or no relation to modern Islamic Iran. (43)

The same sort of nationalism espoused by the constitutionalists at the beginning of the century—urban-centered, Persian-dominated, anti-clerical, finding in its pre-Islamic heritage a source of cultural pride, yet Western-oriented—was continued by the Pahlavi regime. Pre-Islamic Iran, Zoroastrianism and the 'genius of the Aryan race' were glorified, and the Arab Muslims reviled for bringing about Iran's decline from that pre-Islamic greatness. The position and role of Islam and the clergy in society was reduced. Iranian culture was presented as continuing unbroken from pre-Islamic times to the present, and the image of a 'resurgent' Iran was created. (44)

In the 1930s, as the regime drew upon current intellectual notions in formulating its ideological policy, some of the same values came to be shared by writers and the Pahlavi government. Writers such as Ahmad Kasravi (1890-1946), prominent political writer of the time, championed secular nationalism. (45) However, while Kasravi argued for unification into a modern, Persian-speaking Iran, he did not espouse anti-Arabism, noting in his writings that Iran had been independent of the Arabs since the tenth century CE, and asserting that Iranians had willingly accepted Arab Muslim culture, failing to support movements to overthrow the first centuries of Arab rule. (46) Historical novels, recounting the supposed glories of pre-Islamic Iran, were popular, and the condemnation of Shi'i Islam continued as a major theme of modern Persian literature, up to the end of the Pahlavi regime in 1979. (47)

Central to the regime's ideology was the Persian language as a basis for patriotic sentiment and cultural pride, and as a means of national unification.   Here again, in formulating and implementing language policies, the regime was in step with the intellectual trends of the time, for the Persian language had been a subject for concern and debate since the turn of the century, and indeed an important part of the larger debate concerning Iranian national identity.

The Pahlavi regime intended to change the ethnic identity of non-Persian peoples in Iran, making them part of a modern "Iranian" nation held together by Persian language and culture. (48) Persian, the official language of Iran, was used almost exclusively in government and the media.   To the same end, education was placed under government control, centralized and secularized, and among its aims were to propagate Iranian nationalist sentiment and to Persianize Iran.   Persian was designated the official language of instruction, and Persian literature, promoted as the national culture, and the history of ancient Iran were made required subjects. (49)

Another aspect of Persianization was the policy of language reform initiated by Rezâ Shâh along roughly the same lines as the language reform movement in Turkey under Kemâl Ataturk.   In 1935 Rezâ Shâh founded the *farhangestân*, or cultural academy.   Its purpose was to advance the Persian language and literature, with an emphasis on the "purification" of Persian: it issued lists of new Persian words, rediscovered or newly fabricated, to replace foreign words, especially of Arabic origin.   Some individuals published books and newspapers in almost unintelligible "pure" Persian, *fârsi-ye sare*. (50) Geographical names were changed, especially Arabic and Turkish names: Baluchestân became Mokrân; Sowejbolagh, Mahâbâd; Urumieh, Rezâiyeh; Mohammerah, Khorramshahr; and Qamishle, Nayistân. (51) Personal names were also affected, as parents were encouraged to give their children historical or literary Persian names, the usage of which had been limited to the Zoroastrian community. (52) Rezâ Shâh took the last name of Pahlavi, the name of the Middle Persian language, and after 1934, the country was officially designated abroad as "Iran," the "birthplace of the Aryan race," rather than the traditional "Persia," following a suggestion originating from the Iranian Embassy in Berlin. (53) Of course the name "Iran" had always been used in Iran itself, but its use abroad had a different connotation, in light of the official Aryan ideology of Nazi Germany.

Yet, during the Pahlavi period, Arabic remained an honorable major at Iranian universities, and students majoring in Persian literature or philosophy had to know Arabic well.   High school students were required to take six years of Arabic, and elementary students learned to pray in Arabic in the third grade.

The issue of foreign borrowings in Persian, from Arabic or French (and later from English), clearly is not only a linguistic but also a social and political issue. The greatest and most obvious borrowing has been from Arabic, with more than sixty percent of the vocabulary in Modern Standard Persian of Arabic origin; this reflects and may also emphasize the role of Islam in Iranian life. Arabic borrowings in Persian as opposed to more recent European borrowings are one aspect of the conflict between religion and secularization, and tradition and modernization. Thus, the issue of language reform in Iran, and calls for reducing the number of foreign borrowings or converting to the Latin alphabet, have religious and political implications in the debate over modernization, secularization, and nationalism. (54)

Mohammad Rezâ Shâh replaced his father in 1941, when the joint British-Soviet invasion of Iran forced Rezâ Shâh into exile. Mohammad Rezâ Shâh developed a dependent capitalist economy in Iran, as well as extensive ties to the United States after 1953. In other areas, though, there was little change in national policy from father to son; the Shâh continued the centralization of power in Tehrân and its rule over all of Iran, the building of a massive armed force, the suppression of national minorities, and the propagation of "Aryan" ideology. The Shâh reactivated the Academy of the Iranian Language, *farhangestân-e zabân-e Irân*, after the Second World War; the military required official communications to be written in "pure" Persian, and lists of words were circulated to universities for use in their official correspondence up until 1979. (55)

Iranian society, however, was changing enormously. According to Dorraj,

> Iranian society underwent a cultural renaissance in the 1960s and 1970s similar to the changes in political atmosphere that preceded the Constitutional Revolution. New literary and political trends began to appear.
>
> With the blow to national pride after the 1953 coup d'etat, nationalist sentiment intensified. The reaction to Western encroachment took on a more extreme character, and, at this crossroads of history, the preoccupation with the question of cultural and national identity once again became the primary political issue of concern. (56)

The nationalism of the 1960s and 1970s, however, was very different from that of the beginning of the century. While Constitutionalist leaders like Âkhondzâdeh and Kermâni were anti-

Islamic, anti-Arab and pro-Western, the most influential of the new intellectuals, Âl-e Ahmad and Ali Shari'ati (1933-1977), were anti-Western and pro-Islamic. (57) Dorraj gives reasons for the change:

> During the constitutional era, the backward absolutism of the decrepit Qajar state was considered to be the source of poverty, under-development, and social justice. It was hoped that creation of a constitution would modernize the state and curb the arbitrary, repressive rule of the king. During the Pahlavi dynasty, however, coercion was exerted through a "modern" state that had very little respect for the Islamic culture of the country, adopting a hollow version of Western culture and counterposing it to Islamic culture. Therefore, a return to Islam became, on the one hand, a symbolic gesture to refute the culture of the Westernized elite and, on the other, it projected the hopes of reviving the perceived egalitarianism, virtuous piety, and social harmony of the pristine Islamic community. (58)

Now, instead of the Arab, it was the Western Other which was set against the Iranian Self. According to Dorraj,

> The rapid expansion of Western economic and cultural influence in Iran played a decisive role in this turn of events. Devoid of indigenous cultural context, the penetration of Western culture designed to Westernize Iranians ultimately produced the opposite effect. In pursuit of self-assertion, many Iranians reached deep within and revived their cultural identity, Shi'ism. (59)

Dorraj's recognition of Shi'i Islam as part of Iranian cultural identity is another definition of Iranianness, one very different from that of Meskoob. Yet it is a definition which most Iranians have accepted, and which led to the establishment of the Islamic Republic of Iran in the spring of 1979.

With the Islamic Republic came some changes in official policy relating to national minorities. The Constitution of the Islamic Republic of Iran states:

> The official and common language and script of the people of Iran is Persian. All official documents, correspondence and publications, as well as textbooks, must be in this language and script. However, the use of regional and national languages in the press and mass media, as well as

for teaching in schools the literatures written in them, is permitted in addition to Persian. (Article 15)

Since the language of the Quran and of Islamic learning and culture is Arabic, and since Persian literature has been thoroughly permeated by this language, it must be taught in all classes from elementary school through middle school, and in all areas of study. (Article 16)

All people of Iran enjoy equal rights, whatever their ethnic group or tribe, and factors such as color, race and language do not bestow any privilege. (Article 19) (60)

At the same time, the Islamic Republic strongly suppressed political movements by Arabs, Baluch, Kurds and Turkomans in the early 1980s.

Arabs and Iranians

The problem of defining "Persian" or "Iranian" is equally complicated, for there is another side: the problem of defining "Arab." As was noted earlier, there is a certain amount of popular Iranian anti-Arabism. References to Arabs as "*pâ pati*" [barefooted], or "*malakhkhor*" [locust-eating] are common.

Dehkhodâ's *Loghatnâmeh* defines "Arab" largely in terms of race, as "a Semitic people, either city dwellers or others; a group of people different from *'ajam* by which is meant anyone who is not an Arab, such as Fars, Turk, European; the inhabitants of the Arabian peninsula, the Levant, Sudan and North Africa." (61) The *Loghatnâmeh* characterizes Arabs as "taking pride in their past and in their race" and "like all backward peoples." (62)

In contrast, Dehkhodâ defines "Persian" [*fârs*] as "one whose language is Persian [*fârsi*]; one who belongs to the people of Iran [*ân ke az mardom-e irân ast*]; as opposed to Turk, Arab, and others. (63) He defines "Iranian" [*irâni*] as "from Iran [*ahl-e irân*]; citizen [*tâbe'e*] of Iran." (64) These definitions imply that Persian and Iranian are not coterminous. Turks and Arabs can be Iranians, but are not Persians [*fârs*].

Arabs within the borders of Iran are a minority concentrated in the southwest of the country. Even in their home region of Khuzestân, Arabs have experienced great ethnic and professional segregation from Persians, many of whom have been encouraged to relocate there, and who predominate in white-collar occupations. (65) Many Iranians elsewhere in the country may not even know that there are Arabs in

Iran. But most Iranians have had contact with Arabs in Iraq and Saudi Arabia, when they have made pilgrimages there.

Historically, religiously and culturally, however, Arabs have had great importance for Iran. In the seventh century CE, Iran was conquered by Muslim Arabs and made part of the Islamic Caliphate. After the establishment of the Achaemenid monarchy and the flowering of Persian culture, the advent of Islam in Iran was the single most powerful influence on the development of Iranian culture. (66) Iran was changed from a Zoroastrian land to an Islamic one, and Persian language and literature was greatly changed by Arabic, the original language of Islam and of the Islamic caliphate, and Arabic poetic forms. Yet, while Iran was Islamicized, it was not Arabicized. According to Meskoob,

> Finally after four hundred years, Iranians became a nation with a separate identity special to themselves by means of a return to the past, to their own history and with the establishment of Iranian governments and reliance on the Persian language. A new people with a new religion and civilization had emerged with awareness of their own identity. The past was the refuge for this identity and language its stage. Iran was a new tree, nurtured in the climate of Islam, but growing in the soil of its own national memory. (67)

As seen earlier, Meskoob bases his definition of Iranianness on Persian language and pre-Islamic history. Dorraj, however, finds Shi'i Islam to be essential to Iranianness:

> Throughout history, Iranians have had to adapt to the cultures of invading conquerors (Greeks, Arabs, Mongols, Turks, Afghans, and others) in order to survive. Yet, this is only one aspect of the development of Iranian cultural identity. The other dimension of this development is a persistent attempt to forge an identity that is distinctly Iranian. Although the ideological content of this new identity was heavily influenced by the culture of the conquerors, by choosing Shi'ism as opposed to Sunnism, a minority of Iranians opted for a distinct Islamic identity. After a forceful proselytizing process that began in 1501, accentuated by the rise of nationalist consciousness in the late nineteenth century, Shi'ism further solidified its position in Iranian cultural life and became an integral part of Iranian national identity. (68)

Not only does Dorraj see the Iranian Self as Shi'i Muslim, but the ideal Iranian is Ali, son-in-law of the Prophet Mohammad, fourth Islamic Caliph and first Shi'i Imam. According to Dorraj, the image of Ali "has penetrated the Iranian psyche and national consciousness." (69)

> By projecting their idealized self-image onto Ali's character, Iranians have made Ali a symbol of the positive aspects of their national character. In other words, Ali stands for what a good Iranian must be.
> To what extent has Ali become Persianized and to what extent is Iranian culture "Ali-ized"? Perhaps a fair statement of this delicate question is to suggest that Iranians have definitely projected some of their own ideal self-image into Ali's alleged character. One cannot help thinking that behind the idealization and glorification of Ali also lies the nation's psychological need for self-assertion and self-esteem. Throughout history, this nation has been repeatedly overrun and dominated by foreign armies. Its cultural identity has been subjugated to the cultures of invaders and, at times, was forcefully changed, causing Iranians to conceal their true identity and feelings in order to survive. If we add to this picture conditions of general poverty, economic scarcity, and a long history of arbitrary repressive rule by tyrants, then the social ground in which idealization of Ali is rooted becomes clear. In extolling Ali's fortitude and fighting spirit, for example, one also symbolically projects the idea that Iranian "cowardice" was not responsible for the defeats of the past, but rather that the overwhelming military might of the foe or the corruption of the monarchy is to be blamed. Similarly, in Ali's alleged insistence on Islamic principles, such as his unyielding attitude toward favoritism, one can see the psychological need of a nation for a positive self-image in a corrupt society where nepotism is rampant.
> This does not preclude Ali's immense impact in molding Iranian morality, values, and character. (70)

Ali, of course, is an Arab. According to Dorraj, however, "Ali's Arab origins are never discussed. Paintings and portraits of Ali that appear in Iran are those of a handsome Iranian." (71)

Such portraits, however, also look very much like the portraits of Jesus that appear in the West, of a handsome, dark-haired, bearded man wearing Arab-inspired dress; Ali usually wears a *kaffiyah* [traditional Arab headgear] as well. It would be difficult to assign a nationality to either, because, like Jesus, Ali is a religious, not a national, figure; Ali the Muslim is more important than Ali the Arab or Iranian. One could argue that, while Iranians may not see Ali as an

Arab, they do not see him so much as an Iranian either; Ali is simply Ali. An Iranian nationalism based on the Western political model requires defining the Self as Iranian; an Islamic political model may not.

But the "delicate question" raised by Dorraj brings us to another complication, the relationship between Arabs and Islam, and between Shi'i Islam and Iranianness. Iran was Islamicized; in the eyes of some Iranians, Islam is essentially Arab, and therefore non-Iranian. Others, however, hold that Shi'i Islam is an Iranicized Islam, essentially Iranian, and an essential part of Iranianness. Anti-Arab feelings may go hand in hand with anti-Islamic feelings, or one may give rise to the other, or there may be anti-Islamic sentiments without anti-Arab bias, or the reverse. Writers may hold one view or the other; indeed, to some extent, the Pahlavi regime reflected one view, and the Islamic Republic the other.

Finally, the problem in defining "Iranian" comes down to this: within the borders of Iran are many different people who may have little in common, in terms of language, culture and way of life. So what does it mean to be an Iranian? By defining the Arab Other, one can define that Iranian Self, in terms of language, history, race, culture, or religion. We have seen the different definitions of Iranianness articulated by Meskoob and Dorraj. Meskoob's Iranianness is based on Persian language and pre-Islamic history; the Iranian Self is set against the Arab Other. Dorraj, however, sees Shi'i Islam as an essential part of Iranianness; the Iranian Self is set against the Western Other. We shall see how, in defining the Iranian Self, the Arab Other is treated in literary discourse.

Notes

1. Naser Sharify, *Cataloging of Persian Works* (Chicago: American Library Association, 1959).

2. M. R. Ghanoonparvar, *In a Persian Mirror: Images of the West and Westerners in Iranian Fiction* (Austin: University of Texas Press, 1993). See also Mehrzâd Boroujerdi, *Iranian Intellectuals and the West: A Study in Orientalism in Reverse* (Albany: State University of New York Press, 1993).

3. Michael Craig Hillmann, "Revolution, Islam and Contemporary Persian Literature," *Iran: Essays on a Revolution in the Making,* edited by Ahmad Jabbari and Robert Olson (Costa Mesa, CA: Mazdâ, 1981), p. 133.

4. Manochehr Dorraj, *From Zarathustra to Khomeini: Populism and Dissent in Iran* (Boulder, CO: Lynne Rienner, 1990), p. 116.
5. Michael Craig Hillmann, "The Modernist Trend in Persian Literature and Its Social Impact," *Iranian Studies* 15 (1982): 16.
6. Ibid., pp. 15-16.
7. Jalâl Âl-e Ahmad, "Ziyârat" [The Pilgrimage], *Did o Bâzdid* [Exchange of Visits], fifth printing (Tehrân: Amir Kabir, 1970), pp. 37-54; translated by Henry D. G. Law, *Iranian Society: An Anthology of Writings by Jalâl Al-e Ahmad,* compiled and edited by Michael Craig Hillmann (Costa Mesa, CA: Mazdâ, 1982), p. 36.
8. Michael Craig Hillmann, "Iranian Nationalism and Modernist Persian Literature," *Essays on Nationalism and Asian Literatures,* edited by Michael Craig Hillmann, *Literature East and West* 23 (1987): 75-76.
9. Hillmann, "The Modernist Trend," p. 19.
10. Shâhrokh Meskoob, *Melliyat va Zabân* [Iranian Nationality and the Persian Language], second edition (Paris: Khâvarân, 1989); translated by Michael Craig Hillmann (Washington, DC: Mage Publishers, 1992), p. 39.
11. Hassan Kamshad, *Modern Persian Prose Literature* (Cambridge: Cambridge University Press, 1966), p. 39.
12. Richard Weekes, *Muslim Peoples: A World Ethnographic Survey* (Westport, CT: Greenwood Press, 1978), p. xvi.
13. Ali Asghar Hekmat, "Some Aspects of Modern Iran," *Islamic Culture* 31 (1957; reprint edition, New York: Johnson Reprint Corp., 1971): 90-92.
14. Malcolm E. Yapp, "1900-1921: The Last Years of the Qajar Dynasty," *Twentieth-Century Iran,* edited by Hossein Amirsadeghi (New York: Holmes and Meier, 1977), p. 2.
15. Yapp, "1900-1921," p. 16; Fred Halliday, *Iran: Dictatorship and Development* (New York: Penguin Books, 1979), p. 23.
16. Fath Ali Âkhondzâdeh, *Seh Maktub* [Three Writings], unpublished MS, Melli Library, Tehrân; and Mirzâ Âqâ Khân Kermâni, *Seh Maktub,* unpublished MS, in the possession of Prof. Nikki R. Keddie, UCLA; cited by Mangol Bayat-Philipp, "A Phoenix Too Frequent: Historical Continuity in Modern Iranian Thought," *Asian and African Studies* 12 (1978): 205-207.
17. Dorraj, *From Zarathustra to Khomeini,* p. 96.
18. Bayat-Philipp, "A Phoenix Too Frequent," p. 208.
19. Leon Poliakov, *The Aryan Myth: A History of Racist and Nationalist Ideas in Europe,* translated by Edmund Howard (New York: Meridian, 1977), p. 47.
20. Kamshad, *Modern Persian Prose Literature,* pp. 31-53.
21. Mangol Bayat-Philipp, "Tradition and Change in Iranian Socio-Religious Thought," *Modern Iran: The Dialectics of Continuity and Change,* edited by Michael E. Bonine and Nikki R. Keddie (Albany: State University of New York Press, 1981), p. 52.

22. Ferdowsi, *Shâhnâmeh* [The Epic of the Kings], translated by Reuben Levy (Chicago: University of Chicago Press, 1967), p. 415.

23. Ibid., pp. 11-16.

24. Ibid., p. 11.

25. Ibid., pp. 296-97.

26. Nâser Khosrow, *Safarnâmeh* [Book of Travels] (Tehrân: Ketâbhâ-ye Jibi, 1977); translated by W. M. Thackston, Jr., *Nâser-e Khosraw's Book of Travels* (Albany, NY: Bibliotheca Persica, 1986), pp. 82-85.

27. Bayat-Philipp, "Tradition and Change," p. 51.

28. Poliakov, *The Aryan Myth*, pp. 255, 212.

29. Ibid., p. 145.

30. Jalal Al-e Ahmad, *Gharbzadegi* [Plagued by the West], translated by Paul Sprachman (Delmar, NY: Caravan Books, 1982), p. 74.

31. George L. Mosse, *Toward the Final Solution: A History of European Racism* (New York: Howard Fertig, 1978), pp. 51-56.

32. Poliakov, *The Aryan Myth*, p. 73.

33. Ibid., pp. 188-196, 327.

34. Ibid., p. 101.

35. Mosse, *Toward the Final Solution*, pp. 35-38.

36. Gordon W. Allport, *The Nature of Prejudice* (Cambridge, MA: Addison-Wesley, 1954), pp. 107, 113-14.

37. Poliakov, *The Aryan Myth*, p. 47.

38. Halliday, *Iran*, p. 23; Alessandro Bausani, *The Persians*, translated by J. B. Donne (London: Elek Books Limited, 1971), p. 176.

39. E. Sunderland, "Pastoralism, Nomadism and the Social Anthropology of Iran," *The Cambridge History of Iran, Vol. 1: The Land of Iran*, edited by W. B. Fisher (Cambridge: Cambridge University Press, 1968), p. 642.

40. Pierre Oberling, *The Qashqa'i Nomads of Fars* (The Hague: Mouton, 1974), pp. 151-152.

41. Robert E. Looney, *The Economic Development of Iran* (New York: Praeger, 1973), p. 130; Halliday, *Iran*, pp. 176-177; Robert Graham, *Iran: The Illusion of Power* (New York: St. Martin's Press, 1979), p. 27.

42. Bausani, *The Persians*, p. 177; Halliday, *Iran*, p. 23.

43. Bausani, *The Persians*, p. 177.

44. Bayat-Philipp, "A Phoenix Too Frequent," pp. 209-211; Nikki R. Keddie, *Iran: Religion, Politics and Society* (Totowa, NJ: Frank Cass, 1980), p. 99.

45. Bayat-Philipp, "Tradition and Change," p. 52.

46. Ahmad Kasravi, "Irân va Eslâm" [Iran and Islam], *Paymân* 1, no. 8 (February 1933): 9-14; and *Zabân-e Fârsi* [The Persian Language], third edition (Tehrân: 1955), pp. 3-5; cited by Ervand Abrahamian, "Kasravi: The Integrative Nationalist of Iran," *Towards a Modern Iran: Studies in Thought, Politics and Society*, edited by Elie Kedourie and Sylvia G. Haim (Totowa, NJ: Frank Cass, 1980), pp. 111-112.

47. M. R. Ghanoonparvar, *Prophets of Doom: Literature as a Socio-Political Phenomenon in Modern Iran.* (Lanham, MD: University Press of America, 1984), pp. 6-7.

48. Oberling, *The Qashqa'i,* pp. 149-150.

49. Bayat-Philipp, "A Phoenix Too Frequent," pp. 209-210.

50. Mohammad Ali Jazayery, "The Arabic Element in Persian Grammar: A Preliminary Report," *Iran: Journal of the British Institute of Persian Studies* 8 (1970): 122-123; A. Shakoor Ahsan, *Modern Trends in the Persian Language* (Islamabad: Iran-Pakistan Institute of Persian Studies, 1976), p. 114.

51. Wilhelm Eilers, "Educational and Cultural Development in Iran during the Pahlavi Era," *Iran Under the Pahlavis,* edited by George Lenczowski (Stanford: Hoover Institution Press, 1978), p. 321; Henry Field, *Contributions to the Anthropology of Iran* (Chicago: Field Museum of Natural History, 1939), p. 256.

52. Eilers, "Educational and Cultural Development," pp. 321-322; Jazayery, "The Arabic Element in Persian Grammar," pp. 122-123.

53. British Minister to the Foreign Office, "Annual Report for 1934," FO 371/Persia 1945/34-18995; cited by Ervand Abrahamian, *Iran Between Two Revolutions* (Princeton, NJ: Princeton University Press, 1982), p. 143; Donald N. Wilber, *Riza Shah Pahlavi: The Resurrection and Reconstruction of Iran* (Hicksville, NY: Exposition, 1975), pp. 162-163.

54. Michael Craig Hillmann, "Language and Social Distinctions in Iran," *Modern Iran: The Dialectics of Continuity and Change,* edited by Michael E. Bonine and Nikki R. Keddie (Albany: State University of New York Press, 1981), p. 331-32.

55. Ahsan, *Modern Trends in the Persian Language,* p. 131; Halliday, *Iran,* p. 59.

56. Dorraj, *From Zarathustra to Khomeini,* pp. 111-12.

57. Ibid., p. 111.

58. Ibid., pp. 112-13.

59. Ibid., p. 111.

60. *Qânun-e Asâsi-ye Jomhuri-ye Eslâmi-ye Irân* [Constitution of the Islamic Republic of Iran] (n.p.: Omid, 1979), Articles 15, 16 and 19.

61. 'Ali Akbar Dehkhodâ, *Loghatnâmeh,* s.v. "'Arab."

62. Ibid., s.v. "'Arabestân."

63. Ibid., s.v. "Fârs."

64. Ibid., s.v. "Irâni."

65. *Encyclopedia Iranica,* Volume 1, edited by Ehsan Yar-Shater (London, Boston and Henley: Routledge and Kegan Paul, 1985), s.v. "Âbâdân" and "Ahvâz," by X. de Planhol, pp. 51-57 and pp. 688-691.

66. Peter Mansfield, *The Middle East: A Political and Economic Survey,* fifth edition (Oxford: Oxford University Press, 1980), p. 259.

67. Meskoob, *Iranian Nationality and the Persian Language,* p. 38.

68. Dorraj, *From Zarathustra to Khomeini,* p. 10.

69. Ibid., p. 61.

70. Ibid., p. 65.

71. Ibid.

Chapter 2

Men's Writings, Men's Views

Attention now turns to some of the images of Arabs to be found in different works by different writers. Chapter 2 looks at works by five men: fiction writer and essayist Mohammad Ali Jamâlzâdeh (b. 1892); Sâdeq Hedâyat (1903-1951), Iran's most famous 20th century author; short story writer and novelist Sâdeq Chubak (b. 1916); and poets Mehdi Akhavân-e Sâles (1928-1990) and Nâder Nâderpour (b. 1929). With the exception of some poems by Nâderpour, all of the works discussed, in roughly chronological order, were written before the establishment of the Islamic Republic of Iran in 1979. The following chapter looks at women's writings, because the men's views of Arabs, Islam and Iranianness are largely in accord, and very different from the women's views. Chapter 5 explores the reasons for this accord, and difference.

Mohammad Ali Jamâlzâdeh (b. 1892)

Modern Persian prose fiction marks its beginnings with the publication in 1922 of *Yeki Bud Yeki Nabud* [Once Upon a Time], a collection of short stories by Mohammad Ali Jamâlzâdeh. (1) The work is significant as well in that the author, while consciously establishing a new literary style, at the same time addresses the same questions of religion, language and national identity, both in his preface to the work, and in the short story "Fârsi Shekar Ast" [Persian is Sugar]. (2)

The plot of "Persian is Sugar" is simple: the narrator, returning to Iran from abroad, is imprisoned for a short time in the customs house in Enzeli with three other Iranians. The author, however, all the while that the narrator is declaring that all of the other characters too are in fact Iranians, has set things up in such a way as to imply that some of them are in fact more Iranian than others.

The narrator is Iranian. As he explains to the customs officials, "Of course I'm an Iranian. I'm Iranian to the seventh generation. In the whole Sangelaj section of Tehrân, there isn't a single man not acquainted with your humble servant." Being from Tehrân and speaking an educated, standard variety of Persian, the narrator is indubitably Iranian, and the reader is thus persuaded to accept his authority in deciding who is Iranian or not. The young man imprisoned with him, Ramazân, is from Enzeli, and is genuinely Iranian as well; his curses and insults are "as distinctively Iranian as Gorgâb melons and Hakkân tobacco."

But, in contrast to the narrator and Ramazân are the two other characters imprisoned with them, the "Europeanized" gentleman and the mullah. While the narrator himself is returning from Europe, and wearing a derby hat as well, it is "after five years of homelessness and great suffering." Presumably, the narrator is happier in Iran than abroad; perhaps he had even been forced to travel to Europe against his own desires. Thus, even while gaining a certain prestige from his European associations and knowledge (the narrator recognizes that the poem "Mr. Europe" quotes is by Victor Hugo, not Lamartine as Mr. Europe claims), the narrator is still able to represent himself as genuinely Iranian, even in spite of Ramazân's initial assessment of both the narrator and Mr. Europe as Europeans. Ramazân finds the Persian spoken by Mr. Europe incomprehensible, full of French words and phrases, whereas Ramazân realizes that the narrator "really did both understand and speak genuine Persian."

The narrator describes Mr. Europe, with his high collar and novel in hand, as "one of those phony Europeanized types, who could serve as the epitome in Iran of insipidness, foolishness and illiterateness till judgement day." Yet while Mr. Europe is stupid and pretentious, the mullah is bizarre. The Persian spoken by the mullah is full of Arabic words and phrases, and it too is incomprehensible to Ramazân and eventually even to the narrator, who had studied Arabic for a number of years "in the name of formal education." The narrator's description of the mullah and his speech is satirical—the narrator first mistakes him for "a shiny white cat curled up on a bag of coal dust," and "as for the whistling and hissing, it was the sound of his [Arabic] prayers." The narrator continues:

> The mullah would not cease babbling. One would think he had taken an oral purgative or had no power to stop talking. He raised his holy hands from his knees. His arms were unsleeved up to the elbows and from the point of view of hairiness—if you will permit me to say so—resembled sheep's legs. He pushed back his cloak and, using strange and weird signs and gestures, without diverting his fiery and violent look from the spot on the wall, reproached the passport official with the utmost vehemence.

Ramazân's response is to turn to Mr. Europe, saying, "As for the mullah, he has apparently fallen victim to jinns and fits. He doesn't even know our language. In fact, he's an Arab." And later, referring to both the mullah and Mr. Europe, Ramazân declares, "They do not understand a word of human speech; they are both jinns," and, "These madmen do not know a blessed word of real language and all they utter is jinn language."

Both are incomprehensible to Ramazân, because both speak a variety of Persian full of foreign words and phrases, French and Arabic respectively, and in fact Ramazân decides that they are foreigners, a European and an Arab, and jinns and madmen as well. In Ramazân's view, they are literally "foreign devils." To be sure, Ramazân is narrow in his understanding and chauvinist in his views, and one could argue that the author is actually reproaching chauvinism with his satire of one and all. Still, the author's treatment of Ramazân is markedly sympathetic, while his treatment of the mullah and Mr. Europe is not. So, even as the narrator insists that they too are Iranians, the implication is that they and the varieties of Persian they speak are certainly less desirable and less genuinely Iranian, and even less human, tainted as they are by foreign associations, than the characters and languages of the narrator and Ramazân, as different as they are from one another.

Of course, French is not a language native to Iran. Arabic, however, is the language of Islam, the religion of the great majority of Iranians, and there are Iranian Arabs living in southwestern Iran as well, who have been there since before the coming of Islam. (3) Turkish too is spoken in northwestern Iran. The Âzarbâyjâni who arrives as the foursome are being released, however, is not a "Turk" but an "Âzarbâyjâni," who talks "in the peculiar Persian that I later realized was a gift from Istanbul." Ramazân, of course, thinks he is another madman; the narrator knows that "this young man, too, was an Iranian with Persian as his language." Thus, the Âzarbâyjâni speaks neither Turkish nor even Persian full of Turkish borrowings, but Persian with a Turkish accent; he has been suitably Persianized and Iranicized. The mullah and Mr. Europe, however, remain suspiciously foreign, more Arab and European than Iranian.

Jamâlzâdeh's characterization of the mullah is entirely negative. Jamâlzâdeh's satire is anti-clerical, although not anti-Islamic. Yet the story is structured so that the mullah functions not only as a clerical figure but also as a foreign figure, and counterpart to "Mr. Europe." While the depiction of the mullah as a madman and a jinn certainly reduces his religious stature, it clearly seems as well to be an element in Ramazân's assessment of him as an "Arab"; and it is his "Arabness" rather than his religious role that Ramazân finds objectionable. Jamâlzâdeh faults the mullah's lack of understanding of Ramazân's situation, and his insistence on quoting Arabic to him.

According to Hassan Kamshad, Jamâlzâdeh's works are generally critical of Islamic institutions: "it is not, he believes, that the institution they represent is evil, but that the clergy themselves fall short of its ideals and requirements." (4) Indeed, Jamâlzâdeh's father was a pro-constitutionalist cleric, who was assassinated, and Jamâlzâdeh is a *sayyed*, a descendant of the Prophet Mohammad. (5) Jamâlzâdeh criticizes not Islam, but what he regards as clerical backwardness and religious superstition. But Jamâlzâdeh's feelings toward Islam and Arabs are mixed, as can be seen in the memoirs of his childhood *Sar o Tah-e Yek Karbâs* [Cut from the Same Cloth] (1956).

Jamâlzâdeh's recollection of a mob killing two men accused of being Bâbis is a condemnation of religious fanaticism:

> The orthodox and pious men, with a savagery and lack of pity which still after forty years makes my body tremble at the mention, dragged them toward the King's Mosque, that seat of justice and equity for the supreme Islamic law. Meanwhile, an individual came up with a can of oil in one hand and a tin dipper in the other. In a wink, a fire rose toward the sky from the heads and bodies of the two men. Each of the riffraff with righteous piety bought a dipper of that oil for a hundred dinars and sprinkled it over those two faces. (6)

At the same time, Jamâlzâdeh presents the reader with the character of the Sufi "Mowlânâ," an Iranian Muslim of piety and wisdom who has no use for institutionalized religion.

Certainly Jamâlzâdeh was exposed to some popular anti-Arabism. He refers without comment to the popular saying, "The Arab in the desert eats locusts; the dog of Isfahan drinks ice water." (7) More interesting is the image of Arabs as backward and cruel that he internalized as a child:

> It was at one of the sessions of Hâji Âkhond's class in the courtyard of that very school where I first earned a closer acquaintance with the Arabic, "he beat," and "he is beating." From that hour on, I became a source of viciousness along with the other students and our business day and night was to strike and beat the Zayds, Amrs, Bakrs and Khâleds of traditional Arabic grammars. I will never forget when we reached the Arabic "beat," third person plural feminine past, and Hâji Âkhond explained the meaning for us in Persian like this, "They beat, a group of women, third person, in past time." In that childhood world, I saw a handful of Arab women burnt black, all with long Arab clothing, bareheaded and barefooted in the middle of a barren desert, long bamboo poles in hand, attacking a group of weak and miserable men and with the poles going up and coming down, they were beating them as cruelly as possible without its being clear why they were beating or whom they were beating or until when they would beat and even after a lifetime, that same scenery and that same act still materialize before my eyes just at hearing the words "he beat" and "he is beating" in Arabic. (8)

Clearly Arabs and Arabic are closely bound in Jamâlzâdeh's mind, yet Arabic can also have a neutral quality, in the mouth of Mowlânâ, where wisdom can transcend language, just as mysticism transcends religion:

> "Our poets and great men have spoken in this vein in a hundred ways," said Mowlânâ. "Sâ'eb said similar things elsewhere and Niyâz of Shirâz said in the last century,
>   They face the goal from the cloister and the forbidden,
>   The ascetic by one road, the tavern elder by another.
> And someone else has said,
>   The roads toward the Kaaba are many,
>   I go by sea, you by land.
> And the Arabs have said in Arabic, 'Our explanations are diverse and Thy beauty unique'." (9)

It is also clear, that although he is himself a *sayyed*, Jamâlzâdeh does not consider himself to be in any way an Arab. In recounting a visit to a *zurkhâneh* [a traditional sort of gymnasium], Jamâlzâdeh describes the athletes greeting one another:

> They completed the greetings and blessings in nonstop
> succession in the name of *Arab and non-Arab sayyeds,* for the
> glory of the sons of Adam and Mohammad, Moon of Mecca
> and the Holy Place, and in memory of Ali, Eyebrow of the
> Moon of the Bani Hâshem and the Full Moon of our Eleven
> Imams. (emphasis added) (10)

Indeed, Jamâlzâdeh seems to regard Islam as an integral part of Iranian
culture. His objection is to a non-Iranian, backward Islam, as
represented by the mullah in "Persian is Sugar," and reflected in that
story's underlying concern with determining Iranianness.

In his Preface to *Yeki Bud Yeki Nabud*, Jamâlzâdeh discusses the
reasons for his new literary style, one which aimed to reform the
literary language, and to establish a modern literary Persian.
Jamâlzâdeh was hardly alone in his concern with language, for at the
beginning of the twentieth century, the state of the Persian language
was in flux. (11) With the spread of literacy and the press, there was a
need for a new, more popular literary language to fill a role that the
courtly literary tradition could not; Jamâlzâdeh complains, however,
that "men of letters, while composing, still write the masses off, and
continue to produce writings which are obscure and difficult for the
common man to comprehend." (12) According to Jamâlzâdeh, not only
will novels written in "the current and ordinary language of the man on
the street" revitalize Persian literature, but such writing will also
revitalize Iran:

> The novel informs and acquaints various groups of a nation
> with one another: the city-dweller with the villager, the
> serving man with the shopkeeper, the Kurd with the Baluch,
> the Qashqa'i with the Gilak, the Orthodox with the Sufi, the
> Sufi with the Zoroastrian, the Zoroastrian with the Babi, the
> theology student with the athlete, the civil servant with the
> businessman, and in so doing removes and eradicates many
> thousand differences and biased antagonisms which are born
> out of ignorance and lack of knowledge and information. (13)

Jamâlzâdeh thus envisions Iranians eagerly reading popular novels and
at the same time integrating themselves both linguistically and
culturally into a modern Iranian nation; modern literary Persian was to
break down both linguistic and class distinctions.

Jamâlzâdeh is aware of different "groups" in Iran, yet apparently
assumes that all Iranians speak Persian, just different varieties with
various amounts of Kurdish, Turkish, and so on, mixed in. The logical

assumption, then, is that those who do not speak some variety of Persian are not Iranians but foreigners.

Jamâlzâdeh uses a Western model for Iranian nationalism, and sets the goal of a common language and identity, as Persian Iranians, against chauvinism and backwardness. Islam, too, is part of Jamâlzâdeh's definition of Iranianness. However, "Persian is Sugar" suggests that, just as Mr. Europe represents a superficial modernity, the "Arab" mullah represents religious superstition, neither of which will help Iran to progress. Thus, Jamâlzâdeh associates an Arab Other with religious superstition and backwardness, and enjoins the Iranian Self, defined as Persian and Muslim, toward nation-building and modernity.

Sâdeq Hedâyat (1903-1951)

Sâdeq Hedâyat, the most well-known and controversial modern Iranian author, was interested not only in imaginative literature, but also in Iranian history, folklore and culture. He was especially concerned with pre-Islamic Iran, and he studied Middle Persian and translated Zoroastrian texts. The themes of Iranianness, Islam and Arabs are central to many of his works.

Like most modern writers, Hedâyat criticizes the institutions of Shi'i Islam in many of his writings. His criticism is aimed at many different aspects, not only the easier issue of hypocrisy, but also psychological violence and even cruelty to animals.

Alaviyeh Khânom (1933) reveals the moral bankruptcy of a group of pilgrims on their way to Mashhad. (14) Alaviyeh Khânom, herself a *sayyed*, makes her living by taking a religious folk show on the road, displaying painted canvases depicting the martyrdom of Hosayn at Karbalâ while a young man narrates the events. The relationship of the narrator to Alavieyh Khânom is unclear; she introduces him as her son, her son-in-law, and her adopted brother. With them is a twelve-year-old girl, who has already been married three times as a *sigheh* [contract wife], all arranged by Alaviyeh Khânom; she is referred to as her daughter, or her daughter-in-law. There are two other small children with them, whom Alavieh Khânom hits and curses. It is also unclear whose children they are, as Alaviyeh Khânom calls them her children, her grandchildren, or foundlings. In the course of the journey, it comes out that Alaviyeh Khânom has slept with another one of the pilgrims, while both of them have contracted temporary marriages to others. In short, Alaviyeh Khânom is revealed to be a panderer and a whore, as well as hypocritical, cruel, dishonest and ugly. Her conduct is especially reprehensible as a descendant of the

Prophet, and casts doubt on the reliability of such lineage as well. The story is more than an attack on religious hypocrisy; Hedâyat offers no positive religious images, only Alaviyeh Khânom and the rest of the stupid, superstitious characters as representative of Islam.

"Talab-e Âmorzesh" [Seeking Forgiveness] (1932) (15) is another such story. In it a seemingly pious group of pilgrims on their way to Karbalâ gradually reveal the reasons for their pilgrimage. One woman had murdered two infant sons of her husband's second wife, and then poisoned the wife as well. She is terrified that her sins will not be forgiven, until the others reassure her. "God bless you, what do you think we've come here for?" asks one, a man who had been a driver, and had robbed and killed a wealthy passenger. Now he was going to Karbalâ to have the stolen money made lawful by a mullah. Another woman, married to her stepsister's husband, had abused her stepsister to the point of crippling her, and then killed her on their way to Karbalâ. They smugly reassure her that, since they have made the pilgrimage, all will be forgiven: "Haven't you heard from the pulpit that as soon as a pilgrim makes up his mind and sets off, even if his sins equal the number of leaves on a tree, he becomes good and pure."

"Sag-e Velgard" [The Stray Dog] (1942) (16) is the story of a terrier, Pat, whose Western owner loses him in Iran. There he is beaten and horribly abused, all in the name of Islam: "It was to please God that they all hurt him. They thought it perfectly natural to earn their place in heaven by humiliating a dog—a creature which their religion had pronounced unclean and cursed, and which had seventy lives."

Most modernist Iranian writers criticize Islam in two ways: one which condemns a failure truly to practice religion, and the other which condemns religion itself. Hassan Kamshad compares Hedâyat and Jamâlzâdeh:

> Unlike Hedâyat, who hates the religious institution as something alien, as part of the evil resulting from the Arab conquest, which suppressed true Iranian ideals, Jamâlzâdeh is, as B. Nikitine suggests, slightly more sympathetic or urbane towards the clergy. For it is not, he believes, that the institution they represent is evil, but that the clergy themselves fall short of its ideals and requirements. It is on the last count that Jamâlzâdeh exposes the clergy to ruthless satire—which is not the same thing as Hedâyat's numbed horror at everything associated with them. (17)

One senses that horror in the short story "Abji Khânom" [The Spinster] (1930) (18). Abji Khânom is an unattractive, unmarried woman: "Abji Khânom was tall, spare, and dark complexioned with thickish lips and jet black hair." Mistreated by her family, she becomes in turn both disagreeable and outwardly religious: "Since she was five years old she had been told that she was plain and would never marry. She felt deprived of the joys of this world and became determined by means of prayers and observing the dictates of religion to ensure her happiness in the other world." When her younger sister marries, Abji Khânom's jealousy becomes unbearable, and she drowns herself in the underground water tank of the house. The story ends with the image of her corpse: "Her jet black tresses, twisted in pigtails, coiled around her neck like a black serpent. Her green dress clung tightly to her body. Her face wore a halo of light and splendor.... She had gone to Paradise." It is an unwholesome image, full of irony, with her green dress—green the color of Islam—and haloed face, and hair like a snake around her neck.

Hedâyat's horror of Islam is clearest in *Buf-e Kur* [The Blind Owl] (1937) (19), his best known and most important work. The story is filled with images of Islam, all of them negative:

> Early each morning a pair of gaunt, consumptive-looking horses are led up to the shop. They have a deep, hollow cough, and their emaciated legs terminated by blunt hoofs give one the feeling that their fingers have been cut off in accordance with some barbarous law and the stumps plunged into boiling oil. (20)

The muezzin's call to prayer "sounded like the cry of a woman—it could have been the bitch—in the pangs of childbirth. Mingled with the cry was the sound of a dog howling." (21) The Quran is read by the odds-and-ends man:

> He always wears a dirty scarf, a Shushtar cloak and an open shirt from which protrude the white hairs on his chest. He has inflamed eyelids which are apparently being eaten away by some stubborn, obtrusive disease. He wears a talisman tied to his arm and he always sits in the same posture. On Thursday evenings he reads aloud from the Quran, revealing his yellow, gappy teeth as he does so. (22)
>
> Two or three days ago when I shrieked out and my wife came and stood in the doorway, I saw, I saw with my own eyes, that her lips bore the imprint of the old man's dirty yellow, decayed teeth, between which he used to recite the Arabic verses of the Quran. (23)
>
> Yes, I had seen on my wife's face the mark of the two dirty, decayed teeth between which he used to recite the Arabic verses of the Quran. (24)

Thus, Hedâyat places the "Arabic verses of the Quran," the literal word of God, in a debased and repugnant mouth.

In *The Blind Owl*, it is not specific abuses committed in the name of Islam, but Islam itself which is condemned as the object of loathing and dread. This sense of horror arises from revulsion toward the Other. *The Blind Owl* is a tale of xenophobia, of fear and hatred of the Arab Other.

According to Elton Daniel, "the narrator presents his characters as Arab, Turkish, and Indo-European archetypes." (25) The odds-and-ends man is never explicitly said to be Arab. But the identity of the odds-and-ends man is that of the Other, and his identification with Islam, in effect, makes him Arab. The same description is used later for the Turkoman father of the bitch: "He was a bent old man, and he was wearing a scarf wrapped around his neck. He burst into a hollow, grating, gooseflesh-raising peal of laughter, of a quality to make the hairs on one's body stand on end." (26) The description is the same for the narrator's uncle or father, and the narrator himself, as he becomes the odds-and-ends man at the end of Part Four. Such a metamorphosis suggests that Iran, identified with Islam, has lost its Iranian identity.

The obverse of xenophobia is nationalism, and so *The Blind Owl* is concerned not only with the Other but also with the Self, defining Iranian, Persian, in opposition to Arab and Turk. The setting of the story is Rayy, one of the oldest Persian cities; at the same time, the narrator says he doesn't know whether he is in Nishapur or Balkh or Benares. The trend is toward the east, toward India, "a land of mystery, of ancient civilisation." (27); and the cities of Iran and India are said to be essentially the same. Furthermore, this very Indo-European character, the Persian narrator, has an Indian mother, the temple dancer Bugam Dasi, marking the connection between the two "Aryan" nations, Iran and India. It is significant that Bugam Dasi is the only character named in the story; the identity of India is fixed, while the identity of Iran is lost as the narrator becomes the odds-and-ends man, whose identity is fixed not as Self but as Other, as he appears chameleon-like in the guise of the father, uncle, father-in-law, and finally the narrator.

The xenophobia of *The Blind Owl* appears in other of Hedâyat's works. In "Dâsh Âkol" (1932) (28) he describes Iranian Jews:

> He [Dâsh Âkol] walked with long, careless strides past the house of Mullah Eshâq, the Jewish distiller. Without hesitation he entered by the damp brick walk into an old smoke-stained courtyard. Around him were small, dirty rooms with shattered windowpanes, like so many beehives. Green

moss floated on the water of the pool, and the rancid smell of the old cellars permeated the air. Mullah Eshâq, in a dirty nightcap, with a goatlike beard and greedy eyes, came out and forced a laugh.

Mullah Eshâq's son, a filthy, sick-looking child with protruding stomach, stared at Dâsh Âkol. His mouth hung open and saliva dripped from his lips.

But here, Hedâyat's xenophobia needs to be recognized as anti-Semitism.

Mâshâllâh Âjoudâni points out that, in the literature and nationalism of the Constitutionalist era, the original enemy of Iranian culture and cause of all of Iran's problems is Islam and the Arabs. Hedâyat, however, adds the Jews, their religion and customs, to the list of Iran's enemies. In Hedâyat's view, Arabs and Jews, Islam and Judaism, all belong to the same Semitic race, and are essentially the same. Moreover, Hedâyat's anti-Semitism reflects the influence of the facist ideololgy of Nazi Germany. (29) This Western anti-Semitism informs much of Hedâyat's writing.

"Sâyeh-ye Moghul" [The Mongol's Shadow] (1931) (30) was one of three stories by three different authors which appeared in a volume entitled *'Anirân* [Non-Iranian]. The stories are about the invasion of Iran by Alexander the Great (by Shin Partow), by the Arabs (by Bozorg Alavi), and by the Mongols (by Hedâyat):

Shâhrokh became a different person, all right. Up till then he and a small group of young Iranians who had held onto the ways and beliefs of their ancestors—those who hadn't been corrupted—were plotting the overthrow of Arab rule. At first they welcomed the Mongol advances as a sign of hope, as a fatal threat to the race of Sâm [Semites]. But when the Mongols arrived, when the yellow-skinned race of bloodthirsty savages actually invaded their soil—these sheep trotters anointed with filth, with slanted eyes and grubby faces, who had mastered the art of the sword to perfection, and whose narrow minds envisioned nothing other than riding in hordes, setting fires, butchering and inflicting misery wherever they went—then they knew that no matter what they did... the Mongol was the enemy of all things moving, of man, the enemy of life itself.

But, more than Mongols and Jews, Hedâyat is obsessed with Arabs. He refers to Arabs time and again, and in the most diverse places. In the short story "Zendeh be Gur" [Buried Alive] (1930) (31), the narrator, ill and contemplating suicide in bed in Paris, thinks, "If I were dead they would take me to the Paris mosque and give me over to the godless Arabs, and I would die twice over! I can't stand the sight of them." In *Hâji Âqâ* (1945) (32), the despicable Hâji has equally despicable tastes: "After the news he would tune in to the Arab music, listening with pleasure to brayings like those of a stallion-camel as they emerged from the radio-set, and falling into a state of rapture."

In "Esfahân Nesf-e Jahân" [Esfahân is Half the World] (1932) (33), a sort of walking tour of the city's historic and scenic sites, Hedâyat suddenly remarks:

> It comes to mind that, after the time of the Sâsânids, it was in Esfahân in the Safavid period that architecture, tile work, painting and calligraphy, that the artistic spirit of Iran, achieved strength and perfection. The masterpieces of that time are counted as the best examples of the period after Islam. And that which is known in Europe as Indian, Moghul and Arab art—all of it has been of Iranian invention and creation. Especially the Arabs, that were running barefooted after lizards—no artistic thought could be found in their heads, and that which is known as theirs belongs to other peoples, in the same way that today, too, Arab architecture is a ridiculous imitation of Iranian architecture.

And in the introduction to *Tarâneh'hâ-ye Khayyâm* [Songs of Khayyâm] (1934), Hedâyat represents Omar Khayyâm as sharing his own prejudice: "From his angry laughter [and] allusions to Iran's past, it is apparent that he hates the brigand Arabs and their vulgar ideas from the bottom of his heart." (34)

The virulence of Hedâyat's feelings can best be felt in "Seeking Forgiveness":

> A barefooted Arab with a black face, glaring eyes, and a thin beard, beat the mule's bleeding thigh with a thick iron chain. Now and then he turned around and stared at the women's faces one by one.

> A fearsome mob had formed—ragged Arabs, with stupid faces under fezzes, sly expressions under turbans, henna-dyed beards and nails, and shaved heads, counting rosaries, walking up and down in their sandals and cloaks and pajama trousers. They spoke Persian, babbled Turkish, or Arabic issued from the depth of their throats and from inside their bowels and resounded in the air. [There were] Arab women with tattooed, dirty faces, inflamed eyes, and rings through

their noses. One of them had pushed half her black breast into the mouth of the dirty baby in her arms.

In front of a coffee house sat an Arab, picking his nose. With his other hand, he rubbed the dirt out from between his toes. His face was covered with flies, and lice crawled all over his head.

The malice here is almost palpable. For Hedâyat, Arabs are diseased, filthy, ugly, stupid, cruel, and shameless; they have "black" skin, inaccurate, but clearly meant as further invective. They have no worth; even their language is inherently repellent, as they are able to "speak" Persian while Arabic "issues from inside their bowels." For Hedâyat, a religion whose shrine belongs to these people could have no value.

According to Ehsan Yarshater,

> A key element of Hedâyat's tormented feelings is his strong, if distorted, sense of nationalism, which at times borders on chauvinism. His attraction to the study of Middle Persian Zoroastrian literature was no doubt motivated by a belief in ancient Persian virtues and a desire to catch glimpses of a past unsullied by the corruption and debasement of alien influences. His pride in the Persian past and his belief in a glorious ancient Iran can be seen in *Parvin, Daughter of Sâsân*, a drama of mawkish sentimentality, which has as its theme the defeat of the Persians at the hands of the invading Arab armies in the seventh century, and the atrocities suffered by noble, cultivated Persians. This emotionally tinged preoccupation with Persia's failed glory runs through many of Hedâyat's works.
>
> Characteristically, however, Hedâyat passes lightly over Iran's historical achievements and past splendors to concentrate on the anger and dejection born of defeat; it is on the blows and injuries received from the Arabs, the Mongols and other invaders of Persia, rather than on Persian conquests and cultural contributions, that he lingers. (35)

While Hedâyat hates the Other, he especially hates the Arab Other, and he hates Islam in large part because it is Arab. The central, tragic fact of Iranian history is, for Hedâyat, the invasion of Iran by the Muslim Arabs, which destroyed the true Iranian identity. According to Carter Bryant,

> Hedâyat believed that the redemption of the Iranian people lay in a return to its Eastern origins and to Zoroastrianism. The Indo-European Aryans (actually arayayan, or Iranian)

were Zoroastrians, supposed fire worshippers, at the peak of the pre-Islamic Persian golden age. Then, in the middle of the seventh century AD, the Arabs brought Islam, essentially a Western religion, onto the Iranian plateau. Even under the Arabs the Persians managed to retain much of their language and culture. But even when Arab influence weakened, Islam remained; and ultimately, the influence of the Western powers became pervasive. Hedâyat believed that Eastern mysticism, whether one calls it the golden flower, Tao, or the collective unconscious potential, was the solution for himself, for his nation, and for his race in search of an identity. (36)

Parvin Dokhtar-e Sâsân [Parvin, Daughter of Sâsân] (1930) (37) provides Hedâyat with an opportunity to express and propagate these views.

The play takes place around the year 643 CE in the city of Rayy (Raghâ) near Tehrân. The plot is simple. An old artist and his daughter, Parvin, have stayed behind in Rayy while everyone else has fled before the approaching Arab army. Parvin's fiancé, Parviz, manages to visit them briefly before returning to the front. Four Arabs break into the house, kill the dog, loot the house, kill the servant, and drag Parvin from her dying father's arms. Parvin is taken captive and sold to the Arab leader, who asks her, through an interpreter, to accept Islam and become his wife. Parvin refuses, and discovers from the interpreter that Parviz has been killed in battle. Left alone, Parvin is visited by the ghost of Parviz. The Arab leader returns, and as he makes advances toward Parvin, she steals his dagger and kills herself.

From the outset, before any Arab appears on stage, it is made clear that the Arabs are worse than any invading enemy; Parvin's father reflects, "A number of times Iran was the scene of invasions by foreigners. None of them hurt us as much as the Arabs. They have destroyed everything we have, they have robbed, burned and killed." (38) To give these accusations weight, Hedâyat has Parviz give them an eyewitness account of the "bloodthirsty enemy army":

> You don't know what they do, you have to see it, you have to see it.... It is not war, it is butchery. They advance, killing. When they have cut off every head, and their swords are red with blood, they bring fire and burn. They destroy houses, they take women. You have to see it. All of our cities have been leveled, have become a wasteland. Smoke rises from the ruins, and blood flows in streams. (39)

Arabs are repeatedly described as bloodthirsty, savage and cruel: "In order to destroy the Zoroastrian religion, they will not stop at any cruelty or oppression." (40) It is not only the Persians accusing them; later, Hedâyat has the Arab interpreter corroborate the accusations. As he attempts to persuade Parvin to marry the Arab leader, he urges her to think of the people she could help in such a position: "The fate of your fellow believers and countrymen is, to some extent, in your hands. Thousands of men are being tortured, their wives and daughters are to be taken to Baghdad and sold...." (41) The charge of Arabs selling captive women is important; it is repeated throughout the play, and to lend historical credence, there is a footnote, "According to historical documents, the selling of Iranian girls at the hands of the Arabs was customary." (42) No other charges are so substantiated. Sexual violation is both a symbol of the perceived cultural violation of Iran, and the most heinous of those acts of violation.

Hedâyat proceeds literally to demonize Arabs. Parviz calls them "these unwholesome Arabs." The artist damns them as "the enemy of God and a plague"; "it is as though a group of devils and demons thirsty for blood has arisen to destroy the roots of the Iranians." Their invasion has defiled the very soil of Iran: "Our land has been cursed, trampled...; Iran, this heaven on earth, has become a frightening graveyard of Muslims." (43)

Just as Hedâyat dehumanizes Arabs by likening them to demons, and to locusts and plague, he reduces them to animals The servant Bahrâm describes the Arabs he has seen breaking into the house: "Their eyes gleam like predatory animals. They can see in the dark. Their appearance is frightening. They are like monkeys: black, with brutish eyes, dry beards beneath their chins, and ugly voices." (44)

As for the reasons for the invasion, according to Hedâyat, the Arabs wanted to conquer Iran in order to destroy Iranian culture and civilization and to plunder its wealth. Religion is both an excuse for invasion, and a means of destroying Iranian identity.

> They are trying to destroy our language, our belief, and our means of existence, with the excuse of bringing a new religion, and with that excuse they do not keep themselves from any cruelty or oppression. Their intention is conquest, and their armies, like locusts that devour a field of wheat, have poured into our cities.
> The only thing that makes these Arabs victorious is their religion which they fight for. Their leaders have said that if they kill or are killed they will go to heaven. Other than that, their desire is to capture Iranian women, wealth and happiness. They set no limits on their raids and killing. They have seen heaven on earth. These people, who had nothing under the burning Arabian sun except lizards and

dates, have tasted all the pleasures in Iran. They have destroyed towns and farms, cities and countryside.... They have leveled the fire temples. They have burned all our writings because they had nothing themselves. They obliterate our knowledge and our means of existence so that we will have no advantage over them and they will be able to advance their religion more easily among people. (45)

To add insult to injury, these very civilized Iranians are being conquered by "desert-travelling, lizard-eating Arabs, that for years were under our rule and paid tribute to us!" (46) But because the two "races" are so very different, in the end the Iranians will overcome:

No, the Iranian race will not die. We are the same ones that for long years were under the invasion of the Greeks and the Parthians and in the end, we raised our heads. Their language, manners and customs did not suit us. How so, then, with these brutal, naked, barefooted Arabs who have nothing of their own except a long tongue and a sword? (47)

All of this, and Arabs have yet to be seen. Yet when they appear, they meet the expectations created by their description. A loud knocking is heard at the door of the room where Parvin, her father and Bahrâm are waiting, and a voice commands in Arabic, "Open the door, you unclean dogs!" Then, "four Arab individuals enter, swords in hand, heads and faces covered, black, frightening, barefooted and dirty. Their eyes seize upon the girl. The torn cloak of one of them drags on the ground. He holds his bloodstained sword in his hand." (48) The players are described as: "Four Arabs: torn cloaks wrapped around themselves, fastened at their waists with a cord; black faces; rough black beards and moustaches; heads and necks wrapped in dirty white and yellow cloth; dusty bare feet; various swords; brutal, frightening, and they scream and shout." (49)

They speak in Arabic, which of course Parvin and the others do not understand. Hedâyat in a apologetic footnote explains that he has employed Arabic in order not to leave an empty space. (50) The Arabs talk among themselves; they've never seen such a beautiful girl, and their leader will pay them well for her. One of the Arabs picks up a book of drawings, looks at it, throws it on the ground and tramples on it. They roll up the carpet, cut down the silk curtain, and tear the necklace from Parvin's neck. One of them holds her chin in his hand and laughs. When Bahrâm throws himself between the Arab and Parvin, they take him out in the hallway and kill him. Then they drag Parvin, fainting, from her dying father's arms.

The next act opens on the Arab leader, rubbing his hands together in satisfaction as he walks up and down in a room full of loot: boxes of jewels, a throne, silks and carpets. The player is described as:

> Arab leader: short; protruding stomach; thick neck; moustache and beard; a crease between his eyebrows; a long robe, the sleeves of which hang out of his long, simple cloak with piping; a wide shawl; a small dagger at his waist; bare feet; sandals; white pants; black face; frightening; he covers up his inexperience. (51)

The four Arabs enter with a bundle wrapped in white cloth: it is Parvin, still unconscious, as they uncover her before their leader. The Arab leader's eyes gleam; he gulps. He scatters gold Sâsânid coins in front of the four, and they push and shove to pick them up. Then he orders them out.

When Parvin regains consciousness, she wonders if this is not a nightmare. The Arab leader pursues her around the room, telling her in Arabic how lovely she is; when he gets nowhere, he leaves, and returns with an Arab interpreter. The player is described as: "Arab interpreter: 40 years old; wearing *chapiyeh* (*kaffiyah*) and *agal* [Arab headgear], a yellow robe, long white cloak, a shawl, and shoes and socks; he speaks distinctly and intensely." (52) One notices the interpreter's relatively benign appearance, and his shoes; perhaps being with Iranians, learning their language, has to some extent "civilized" him.

The interpreter tells Parvin that the leader has never seen any woman as beautiful as she, and if she will accept Islam, he will cover her with jewels, house her in a palace, and his other wives will be her servants. This is in keeping with the previous accusations of sexual violation, that the Arabs want Iranian women, and is racist: "black" (or Arab) women are not as beautiful or desirable as "white" (or Iranian) women. Furthermore, defending the honor of "white" women against the threatening sexuality of "black" men is a paradigm of racism. "Miscegenation" violates both sexual purity and the racial purity encoded therein.

As the interpreter tries to persuade Parvin to marry the Arab leader, Hedâyat turns their talk into an historic debate, repeating the accusations expressed earlier. The interpreter tells Parvin that it was the will of God that the Arabs should be victorious, and lead the Iranians to the path of righteousness. Parvin retorts, "Your religion is an excuse, your desire is conquest, wealth, stealing and savagery." When the interpreter reminds her of Iran's conquests, of its wars with the Romans, Turânians, and Arabs, she replies, "We were fighting to defend our freedom. We never fought with anyone else in the name of religion, and we did not degrade the religion and customs of others, we left them free."(53)

The destruction of Iranian civilization is again cited, as the interpreter tells her, "After the battle of Nahâvand, your language and religion died." Parvin asks,

> When you burned our books, did you think that that would cause us to adopt your language and your religion? All you achieved was to stain your own name for all eternity. Future generations will curse you, because, out of ignorance and jealousy and insanity, you did not know the value of knowledge, and you burned the memorial of past generations. (54)

He replies that knowledge does not matter, all one needs is to believe and accept. She replies, "Yes, but not blindly. Our religion is one with knowledge." (55)

Parvin tells the interpreter that the Arabs, who have newly come to religion, have no business teaching Iranians, whose religion is ancient. Furthermore, the Arabs' religion is not only new, it is wicked, and suits a savage race:

> The god that you worship is Ahriman, god of war, god of killing, god of vengeance, god of savagery that wants blood. Your actions, your ways and customs are based on torture and degradation. You thirst for people's blood. All of your actions foul the earth and degrade the human race.
> Yes, we began the war because your religion does not suit us Iranians. Maybe it is good for you, because you live like savage animals. It has shown you the right path. But we have understood good and evil for a long time. (56)

Parvin Dokhtar-e Sâsân is a perfect expression of Hedâyat's views. According to Âjoudâni, Hedâyat's nationalism revolves around the axis of blood and race, and the superiority of the Aryan Iranian race. (57) Hedâyat's anti-Arab and anti-Islamic views are part of his larger anti-Semitism. In line with Western racist theory, Hedâyat believes that Iranians and Arabs are two different races, one Aryan, the other Semitic, and one superior to the other. He portrays the Arabs as dark-skinned, savage and inhuman. Hedâyat idealizes the pre-Islamic past as the Golden Age of Iran, but dwells more on the bitterness of its end at the hand of the Arabs. In his understanding of history, Iran's true cultural identity was destroyed by the Arab Muslim invaders, who replaced Iran's superior civilization with the brutal and bloodthirsty culture and religion of their own. He abhors Arabs, and abhors Islam as well, because of its Arab association. It would be difficult to find writing more defamatory or openly racist than that of Hedâyat.

Sâdeq Chubak (b. 1916)

Sâdeq Chubak was born and attended elementary school in the southern town of Bushehr, on the Gulf. He later moved with his family to Shirâz. He also worked for a time as a teacher in Khorramshahr. (58) Because he is from the south, from the Gulf coast, and especially because he lived for some time in Khorramshahr, one might expect to find Arab characters in his works.

By and large, however, Arabs do not appear, with only occasional references to Arabs in passing. "Cherâgh-e Âkhar" [The Last Offering] (1966) (59) is the story of a young man, Javâd, returning by boat to school in India. The boat goes from Bushehr to Basra, then Kuwait, Bahrain and Qatar, and finally Calcutta. It is carrying a varied load of passengers and pilgrims to Karbalâ: "Iranian, Indian, Afghan, Arab, black, white, woman, and child." One of the Iranian pilgrims is overheard saying to another, "No, Basra is cheap. But you have to watch out for your belongings. As soon as you turn your face away, the Arabs will steal your things. There are no thieves worse than Arabs." And in the novel *Tangsir* (1963), the story, based on a true incident, of a Tangestâni man who kills the four Bushehr notables who have cheated him of his life savings, the hero is described as one who "got along with both Arabs and Iranians." (60)

In another short story set in Bushehr, "Monsieur Elias" (1945) (61), the narrator describes the other tenants living in the same house; one of them is a tailor, who "has another wife in the Arab quarter."

Interestingly enough, however, there is a description of the wretched family, so pitied by the protagonist, until it is learned that they have bought the house he rents in:

> There were two little boys without pants, wearing two old, stained shirts that reached to their belly buttons. Their eyelids were red and half closed with trachoma. Between the bloody eyelids, two cloudy pupils, like the clay beads of a rosary, moved from left to right. One of the boys was eating a yellow cucumber and at the same time he was licking the drippings from his nose for the salt. Their heads and faces looked as though they had been playing with soot. Two narrow streams of tears from the corners of their eyes had

mixed with the dirt on their cheeks and dried on their faces. The crooked nose, bulging eyes and straight, cornsilk hair of the mother, and the wide open eyes (like the eyes of a mouse caught in a trap), the round and fleshy face, fat stomach, high wide forehead and bald head of the man of the family, showed without a doubt that this is a Jewish family.

The anti-Semitism evidenced by this passage appears again, in *The Patient Stone*, where it applies to both Jews and Arabs.

While Arabs as such do not much concern Chubak, the theme of Islam and its Arab element does. Much of his writing is sharply critical of the institution of Shi'i Islam in Iran. "The Last Offering" revolves around a Sayyed, who shows paintings of religious scenes and narrates their stories to make a living, and Javâd, who despises the Sayyed and all that he represents:

He was thinking of the Sayyed, of his complaining and his "Oh, Mother, I am far from home," his arrack-drinking, his carelessness, and his greed. It was as though a voice was whispering in his ear, "This work has no effect. The root must be destroyed. A sun shing over the whole world will have to shine on these people's heads to burn the superstitions out of their brains. With this same talk, they destroyed our honor, our nationality, our pride. Wretch. He says, "I am an Iranian," and wants to go for a year to India, China, and beyond China, and bring more shame upon us."

Javâd decides to throw the Sayyed's paintings overboard while he is asleep:

The sleepy, broken sound of "God is great" coming from one of the sleepers made his stomach turn. The canvases in the box rattled and gave off the smell of paint and rancid oil which smelled like camphor, shrouds, graves and Arabic.

Thus Chubak portrays the Sayyed as a hypocrite and a scoundrel, and Islam as base superstition which has destroyed Iran's national honor.

Perhaps even more strongly critical of Islam is the short story "Ba'd as Zohr-e Âkhar-e Pâ'iz" [An Afternoon in Late Autumn] (1945) (62). A teacher is showing the class how to pray, but a little boy named Asghar cannot concentrate on the lesson. The Arabic prayers and terms confuse him, and the prostration reminds him of how Mash Rasul, the baker's apprentice, sodomizes him. His thoughts reveal the utter, desperate poverty of his situation, and, in that context, the religious instruction he receives is meaningless, and religion itself irrelevant.

Chubak's concern with Islam and its Arab element appears again in *Sang-e Sabur* [The Patient Stone] (1966) (63), a fictionalized account of a series of murders which took place in Shiraz in the 1930s. It is a grim and difficult novel, in which several interrelated stories are told through stream of consciousness monologues, first person narration of events, transcription of other works, and plays by the main characters: Seyf al-Qalam, the Indian doctor, who is convinced that it is his religious duty to kill all prostitutes; Gowhar, one of his victims, who was divorced by her husband because he believed their child to have been the result of her adultery, and who now supports herself and Kâkolzari, her son, through religiously sanctioned concubinage; Jahânsoltân, the invalid servant who accompanied Gowhar from her husband's house; Shaykh Mahmud, Gowhar's procurer; Belqays, the landlady and sexually frustrated wife of an opium addict; and Ahmad Âqâ, an impoverished teacher and would-be writer of the stories of the lives of Gowhar and Jahânsoltân. According to M. R. Ghanoonparvar,

> *The Patient Stone* may be the epitome of all Chubak's literary output in that it is an imaginative mosaic in which he brings together all those elements of his earlier works which marked him as a writer of distinction in Iran, particularly his choice of low-life characters, his use of colloquial language, his themes and world view, and his attention to the formal aspects of fiction. (64)

One of the principal themes of *The Patient Stone* is rootlessness, alienation and loneliness. (65) Ahmad Âqâ feels as if he has been thrown into space; he has been disconnected from history, art and tradition. On one level, this is a universal existential problem: Ahmad Âqâ speculates, "I imagine man has always been frightened of loneliness, from the very beginning. I'm lonely too." (66) He wants to find meaning in life, to get to the bottom of things. His double, the spider Â-Seyyed Maluch, answers him: "The bottom of all this can never be found. It's all suffering and torture, migration and separation. And there's no end to human sorrow. Everyone is sitting with their hands folded on their laps waiting for death. Go read Khayyâm. This person was the only being who resolved everything." (67) On another level, however, it is an historically and culturally specific problem, which Ahmad Âqâ faces as an Iranian. He wants to write, to solve his problems, but:

How do I know that my writings won't get buried with me under the rubble? How much has already been buried in the earth since the world began? How much writing has been wiped out? How much of it did the Arabs and Mongols burn and destroy? Where are the Sassanian writings? Where's Rudaki's *Kalileh and Demneh*? Where are Beyhaqi's works? And where are the hundreds of other things whose names we don't even know? I ask you, didn't this country have anything? Did the Achaemenians, the Parthians, and the Sassanians come from under the bush? No books, no art, no economy, no religion, no army, no stories, no poetry, no buildings, nothing? Where are they all? Who destroyed it all? Bastards! The Arabs didn't bring us anything. Whatever we had they destroyed. To hell with it. Maybe we didn't deserve any of it. (68)

According to this view, the Arab Muslim conquest of Iran is the root cause of individual and social alienation and malaise; the Arabs destroyed a great Iranian civilization and could not replace it, and ever since Iranians both individually and socially have suffered because they have had nothing as Iranians, no history, no art, no culture, and no traditions of their own. Even writing, which offers both an existential and social solution, in problematic. Ahmad Âqâ wants to tell the story of Gowhar's life, but there is no Persian literary tradition of realism; if the truth is ugly, it cannot be written. Again, the fault is seen to lie with the Arabs and Arabic, and their influence on Persian language and literature:

Indeed, I do love the literature of the Arabs.... Alas, the public is ignorant, or they would, to illuminate and administer an enema to the Persian language, find no way but to replace the immodest Persian words and diction with Arabic words; in fact, we must strive to the utmost to replace Persian with Arabic words and diction. Ah, surely I have made your dear head ache. This was intended as a love letter, not as a treatise on the superiority and virtuosity of the Arabic tongue over the Persian. I worship the Arabic language.... I was speaking of the writings of Ebn Abi al-Qazib. In this book I read a story of his of which the following is a summary. In Yemen, a Nubian youth tears out with a dagger the seat of the liver of the husband of his beloved. It is a love tale mingled with psychology. You, my lovely, know of the importance of psychology. But you do not know with what chaste refinement and self-restraint it has been written, and all the while it remains a delicate love tale; its learned scribe has not deviated even a jot from the modest path. And although all

matters are certain and clear interlinearly, still, no mention
by name is made of kisses and of that obscene act and those
filthy, immodest, and repugnant words, metaphors, and
allusions which have become the peculiarity of the mutilated
Persian language. Briefly, this youth in love, at night while
his beloved is sleeping in her bed with her husband, kills her
husband with a dagger; and in that very bed which had become
a little pool of blood, he copulates with his beloved. (69)

Ahmad Âqâ's complaint is that Persian has been Arabicized, and
prettified to the point of falsehood; Arabic elements have "mutilated"
the Persian language, and Arabic literary traditions have been imposed
upon Persian to create a literary tradition of hypocrisy which requires
that the ugly truth be written as a beautiful lie. The racism of this
passage is striking: here an Arab writes in elegant Arabic about a
bloodthirsty Nubian man and his equally depraved Yemeni beloved for
an Arab audience which obviously shares a taste for blood, depravity,
and hypocrisy. Thus Arabs are presented as hypocritical and bloodthirsty, while the author reveals his own concern with miscegenation,
between a Semitic Yemeni and a Black Nubian.

History is an important theme in the novel. Ahmad Âqâ returns
to it again and again in search of an answer to his plight. In the midst
of the confusion surrounding him, he transcribes the ending of
Ferdowsi's *Shâhnâmeh*, where Rostam Farrokhzâd foretells the defeat of
the Sâsânid Persians by the Muslim Arabs, and grieves for the future
where only the Arabs will prosper, and Ahriman, the Lie, will rule:

When the pulpit becomes equal the throne,
Names will be Omar and Abu Bakr alone.
All our labors will be in vain,
And our kingdom the unworthy will gain;
Neither throne, nor crown, nor city will survive;
The stars say only the Arabs will thrive.

Honor and truth shall be rejected;
Lies and baseness shall be respected.

True warriors shall they dismount,
And the boastful and vain will surmount.
The fighting gentry shall be cut from the root;
The artful race will bring forth no fruit.

No faith or loyalty in the world will be found;
The tongue and the soul with hatred will be bound.

From Persians, Arabs, and Turks will appear
A race so mingled and so queer —
Nor Turk, nor Arab, nor high-born,
Ideas as playthings shall they scorn.

This Ahriman's day will soon arrive
When the Turning Wheels our fall contrive. (70)

What the Arabs brought to Iran, of course, is Islam, and religion is another important theme in the novel. Chubak sees Islam as a tool for oppression, especially of women. In *The Patient Stone* he condemns the practice of polygamy, a husband's unrestricted right to divorce, and temporary marriage.

Gowhar had been married to Hâji Esmâ'il when she was twelve, and bore his only child, Kâkolzari. His other wives, however, were jealous of her, and accused her of adultery. Hâji Esmâ'il was convinced of his son's illegitimacy when Kâkolzari's nose started bleeding at the shrine of Shâh-e Cherâgh, and he drove his wife and son out of the house, along with Jahânsoltân whom he kicked down the stairs, breaking her back. No one will believe Gowhar and Jahânsoltân who insist that the child was hit in the face by a villager in the crowd at the shrine.

Forced to support herself, Gowhar has turned to religiously sanctioned concubinage. Her procurer is Shaykh Mahmud, who has power of attorney from Gowhar to make her a legal concubine. Ahmad Âqâ asks him to define "legitimization by consent," the means by which her sexual services are made lawful:

I knew myself what filth it was. I saw that even in his preacher's world he was still ashamed to confess that in the twentieth century this kind of stink and filth is still common. He said, "'Legitimization by consent' is such that a person allows another the act of penetration with his concubine slave and this is particular to the saved sect of Twelvers thus at the instant that the owner says that he allows the act of penetration it is legitimized and the interim period is not necessary as a condition either and the concubine slave as soon as she has been bought and owned or the consent for penetration has been given becomes lawful to him even if the concubine slave be a debauchee or the consequence of adultery." My head got hot; I wanted to spit in his face. But was he to blame? (71)

Ahmad Âqâ tells Shaykh Mahmud, "Between you and me, what is this, you capitalizing on this poor woman? You keep renting her to anybody and everybody just like a public outhouse ewer, and then, with a few Arabic sentences you think you make it lawful?" (72)

Later, when he invites Gowhar to come to him, he tells her, "If you're stuck on lawful concubining, go to Sheykh Mahmud. I don't have to empty out my juice to the tune of a male camel groaning." (73) Of course, the characterization of Arabic as sounding like a "male camel groaning" is racist, and needs no further comment. What Ahmad Âqâ finds even more repellent is that Gowhar's concubinage is not only religiously sanctioned, but "is supposedly a good deed, deserving of heavenly reward too." (74)

Ahmad Âqâ remembers, when he had been about the same age as Kâkolzari, how his father had divorced his mother, after she had borne him seven children, and married a second wife, a fourteen-year-old girl, on a trip to Shirâz. His mother is stunned and hurt. His uncle forces his mother and her children to sleep in the storage room, and forcibly goes through their belongings. When his father returns, he has become a stranger to the boy. He tells the boy's mother that they forced him to take another wife, and that it was only a single divorce, which he reverses and so makes her his wife again. (75)

Chubak criticizes the cruelty toward women of men who call themselves Muslims. However, his condemnation of the treatment of women does not distinguish between Islamic precepts and the interpretations and practices of Iranian society. Chubak blames Islam, and the Arabs that brought Islam to Iran.

Gowhar's murderer is an Indian doctor with "a weird name, Doctor Seyyed Vakili Sâheb Seyf al-Qalam. He looks ridiculous. He's a thin, hunched, short-necked sayyid with thick greasy black hair frizzled up on his head." (76) Seyf al-Qalam is another example of miscegenation, perhaps the fulfillment of Rostam Farrokhzâd's prediction: "From Persians, Arabs, and Turks will appear / A race so mingled and so queer." (77)

Seyf al-Qalam describes himself:

> I am a stranger here. I know Persian better than they do; but this stinking Indian accent makes me an object of ridicule for them. I am short in stature. I am ugly. Scrofula has made my face resemble the dead. I am moneyless, and no one pays any attention to me. I am all alone. (78)

He is even more alienated than Ahmad Âqâ, and quite insane. He plans to rid the world of poverty, vice and disease by killing all the prostitutes with cyanide. In the disordered, upside down world of the novel, however, this madman from India is an observant Muslim:

> May Allah forbid, sir. I am not an adulterer, to have
> committed adultery with her, to know whether or not she had
> tattoos on her abdomen. 'I ask Allah Who is my Creator for
> forgiveness, and unto Him do I return.' I, sir, am a Moslem, a
> Twelver Shi'ite. I have struck with my sword for Islam. I am
> proud to say that I have never neglected my prayers and
> fasting. (79)

He is also able to recognize Gowhar's trade for what it really is:

> It makes no difference; Khânom Laqâ brought me women and
> received three *qerâns* for every *tomân*. Sheykh Mahmud
> brought me this woman, receiving about the same, and said
> that he was in this business. I am the enemy of gonorrhea and
> the clap. A temporary concubine is no different from a
> prostitute. (80)

One of the most decent characters in the story is Jahânsoltân, the
servant lying paralyzed in the stable in her own excrement with no one
to care for her. Ahmad Âqâ thinks to himself, "She looks like she
doesn't belong to the living anymore. But she still wants to stay alive.
There's still love in her heart. She loves Gowhar and Kâkolzari. Even
with half her body eaten away by maggots, she's still concerned about
Kâkolzari going hungry." (81)

She is devout, trusting in God's justice. Yet when she dies, it is
in fear and delirium:

> Nakir and Monkar come to the grave with a club of fire. Oh,
> please, I'm a Moslem. Wait. I'm gonna say it right now. It's
> on the tip of my tongue. I'm gonna say it right now. It's
> Arabic, I forgot it. Ow, ow, wait, I'll say it. I heard it a
> thousand times from the preacher on the pulpit. Wait till I
> asks my maggots. Hey, maggots. For the love of God, hurry
> up, answer Nakir and Monkar. *Hurry up, say your testaments*
> *or I'll bust your head open with the club of fire.* (82)

Jahânsoltân is a good Muslim who keeps her prayers, even in her
wretched condition, but Chubak will not allow her to remember the
testament, because it is Arabic, and "foreign" to her as an Iranian.

However, Islam is not the only cause of Ahmad Âqâ's alienation,
or of the misery around him. Ahmad Âqâ finds no answers either in
Persian history or religion, Zoroastrianism, and he begins to
deconstruct them both. Thus, while having sex with Belqays, he tells
her,

> You poor thing, if you'd been born in Arabia, they'd have
> buried you alive because a woman wasn't even worth a mangy
> camel. But, don't you ever forget that in that same day and
> age the monarchs of this country were two women,
> Purândokht and Âzamidokht, and no one ever buried their
> daughters alive. (83)

At first glance, this is common Iranian nationalism, looking back to
the pre-Islamic Golden Age, and anti-Arab chauvinism. But there is a
level of irony here as well, as he says this to the wretched Belqays, poor
frustrated wife of an impotent opium addict. To her it cannot possibly
have any meaning.

Later, Ahmad Âqâ recreates a scene from the life of Ya'qub Leys,
founder of the Saffârid dynasty which ruled in eastern Iran during the 9th
century, who challenged the rule of the Caliph in Baghdad. The
Caliph's envoy appears, with the message that, if he will stop fighting,
he will be allowed to remain the prince of Khorâsân, Sistân and
Kermân. Ya'qub Leys refuses, and the messenger leaves.

The messenger is "a tall, strong Arab. The Arab is dressed in
clothes of gold-embroidered red silk, and is totally unarmed." Ya'qub
tells him, "When you first set foot on this land, you were all naked
beggars whose heels having never had shoes were callused like the
hooves of dromedaries. But now, through the charity of the people of
Persia, you roll in gold and shining silk." When the messenger leaves,
one of Ya'qub's companions asks him, "Did you see with what
expensive ornaments that rat-eating little fellow had adorned himself?"
And Ya'qub refers to "these baser-than-dog Arabs." (84)

Again, this is common anti-Arab nationalism, but there is
another, ironic level of meaning as well: Ya'qub is suffering from colic,
but refuses an enema, as disgraceful, and one of his companions is
named Âzhar Khar (Âzhar the Donkey). Ahmad Âqâ's version of the
story of Anushirvân the Just is even more absurd, with the legendary
Bell of Justice revealed to be only an animal hide, incapable of ringing,
and injustice the rule throughout the land. (85) Ahmad Âqâ goes so far
as to equate Zoroastrianism with Islam:

> In that day and age people were so stupid they worshipped
> fire. But the Sword of Islam busted the hell out of their infidel
> hides. If it weren't for the double-edged Sword of Heydar the
> Impetuous in place of the Black Stone, you and I would now
> have to worship fire too. (86)

Yet Ahmad Âqâ hates the God he has been taught about. While reflecting on Gowhar's life, he defines that God, the God of Islam:

> What else is this woman good for? Always pushed! From the time she could tell her right hand from her left, she's seen a monster inside her watching her, all eyes, and she, like a beggar, with her eyes fixed on his hand hoping to be forgiven for uncommitted sins. A monster who tortures tyrannically and fries man's flesh to a crisp in the sticky fires of Hell. If He feels like it, He forgives and grants salvation. But to forgive, He demands payment. His payment is weeping, moaning and groaning, self-flagellation on the chest and on the back with chains, banners, passion plays and self-laceration. He's the enemy of joy, laughter, and dancing. He hates painting, sculpture, singing and music. He'll damn you if you make a statue out of clay, 'cause you won't be able to give it life on Resurrection Day. He watches you, all eyes, and you can't hide anything from Him. (87)

The final episode of the novel, the Myth of Creation, is the answer to Ahmad Âqâ's question, "What's at the bottom of all this?"

> Once there was a god, Zervân, Time and Fate, who created a world, populating it with many creatures created for mere sport. To one of these, Mashyâ, he gave the power of thought, which became a source of the creature's discontent, his feeling of loneliness. As part of a plot against Zervân, Zervân's assistant Ahriman, the Lie, made use of Mashyâ's discontent, created for him a mate, and together they destroyed the monster god. Ever since, the world has been ruled by Ahriman, the Lie. (88)

Ahmad Âqâ's myth of creation mixes elements from Zoroastrianism, and from the Judaeo-Christian-Islamic tradition, and turns many of the elements upside down. (89) Thus Ahriman, the Lie, is a beautiful fairy, while Zervân, the good creator, is ugly and cruel:

> Zervân is a huge, terrifying monster with a spotted body, two dirty, rusty, curved horns, and fiery eyes. Two dirty, black wings hang from his shoulders and a tail like that of a bull hangs down off the throne. His boar-like fangs stick out from between his lips. He appears rough, hard-hearted, irreconcilable, and speaks with a thick Hebrew accent. (90)

And if there were any question as to who Zervân really is, Chubak answers, as Zervân says to Mashyâneh, "I guess when Ahriman set out to make you, she didn't first invoke the name of God [Allâh]. You are such a chatterbox." (91) In Chubak's Myth of Creation, Zervân has become Allâh, with an explicitly Semitic identity. Chubak makes a Semitic connection between Islam and Judaism, a connection in terms of a racial category, and Zervân turned Semite is cruel and ugly.

The Myth of Creation episode echoes Â-Sayyed Maluch's answer, given at the beginning of the novel, that there are no answers, that life is indeed without meaning: "The bottom of all this can never be found. It's all suffering and torture, migration and separation. And there's no end to human sorrow." Religion offers no answer, but neither does the future without God, as the ambiguous, rather ominous ending of the myth suggests. Chubak rejects Islam as a religion, just as he rejects Zoroastrianism. He rejects Iranian chauvinism as well. Existential despair informs the Self more than categories of Iranianness or Arabness. Yet Chubak also creates characters who reveal racist thinking, and voice Western anti-Semitism. There is a level of anti-Arab sentiment throughout *The Patient Stone*, a level of meaning which is in no way negated by the other, ironic, level. Chubak's characters see an Arab Other, hypocritical, ugly and cruel, and an Iranian Self, defeated and further corrupted by Semitic hypocrisy in the form of Islam, and Chubak seems to hold out little hope for either.

Mehdi Akhavân-e Sâles (1928-1990)

The poet Mehdi Akhavân-e Sâles, like Hedâyat, despises Arabs, and mourns the passing of Iran's pre-Islamic culture and greatness. Born in Mashhad, in Khorâsân province, Akhavân claims not the Islamic city of Mashhad, but the pre-Islamic city of Tus near Mashhad as his rightful birthplace: "I am from Tus and a devotee of Zoroaster/Neither Arab, nor Turk, nor any one of this sort." (92) Two of Akhavân's most famous poems, "Âkhar-e *Shâhnâmeh*" [The Ending of the Shâhnâmeh] (1959) and "Shush râ Didam" [I Saw Susâ] (1972) reflect on Iran's past greatness and present ruin, and the need to come to terms with that history, and a present-day sense of "rootlessness," of "living, as it were, after their time." (93)

"The Ending of the *Shâhnâmeh*" (94) refers to Ferdowsi's epic of mythic Iranian kings and heroes, literally ending with the coming of the Muslim Arabs to Iran. In the poem, "the harp, broken and out of tune," sings of Iran's former greatness:

> We are
> the conquerors of history's fortresses of glory,

> the witnesses of each century's cities of splendor.

The harp dreams of the past:

> It sees itself in the Sun's luminous court
> as the rare beauty and beloved of Zoroaster
> or a coquettish intoxicated fairy
> in the pure bright meadows of moonlight.

But all of that is ended with the coming of the Muslim Arabs. In place of the the pure light of the sun and moon, the harp sees the religion of Islam as:

> false lights —
> the caravan of dead flames in the swamp —
> on the sacred brow of the mihrab.

And now Iranians live in:

> this mad century of false faith
> with its nights bright like day,
> its stark and dark days like nights in the depths of fairy tales
> . . .this turbulent century of evil faith,
> the crooked-faced century
> which has surpassed the moon's orbit,
> but remains so far from the pivot of the sun

The good light of Zoroastrianism has been replaced by the false light of Islam, and the perverted light and dark of the twentieth century, and now:

> We are conquerors of cities gone with the wind.
> In a voice too weak to come out of the chest,
> we are narrators of forgotten tales.

The poem suggests that, for Iranians at least, the ending of the *Shâhnâmeh*, the ending of Zoroastrian Iranian culture with the defeat of Sâsânid Iran and the coming of Islam has resulted in a present-day existence of ruin and despair. But the poem is not entirely hopeless: there is a suggestion of hope in the speaker's telling the harp to "change the tune." (95). More than that, there is a solution implied in the very view of history Akhavân presents: if the past was good, and the present bad, then perhaps one should return to the past.

It is this course of action that Akhavân suggests in the later poem, "I Saw Susa." (96) The ruins of the Achaemenid city recall to the speaker Iran's former greatness:

> this old, dark image of the glory and the grandeur of old Iran,
> second Persepolis, the high Aryan roof of the East.

Then the wind, hissing among the ruins, addresses the present generation:

> 'Either destroy me, level me with the dust,
> sweep me away, or rebuild me, spineless generation, O....'

Clearly, Akhavân sees the pre-Islamic era as Iran's Golden Age, and he suggests returning to the pre-Islamic, Zoroastrian culture which gave rise to such greatness in the past and which supposedly could do so again in the present.

Akhavân makes even more explicit his views elsewhere, most completely in the epilogue to *Az in Avestâ* [From this Avesta] (1965). According to Sorour Soroudi, "Omid is today an outspoken supporter of the view that blames foreigners, mainly the Arabs, for Iran's present predicament, and proposes restoration of and emphasis on pure Iranian elements, Iran's pre-Islamic heritage." (97)

Akhavân's solution is the restoration of the pre-Islamic Indo-Iranian heritage, adapted to the needs of the present, in particular a neo-Zoroastrian religion which embraces not only Zoroaster, but the Sâsânid heretical reformers Mâni and Mazdak, and the Buddha as well. (98) Akhavân's world view "is black and white in the sense of the Zoroastrian dualistic principle of light and darkness represented by Ahura Mazda and Ahriman. Everything connected with ancient Iran and Iranian culture is pure, bright and beautiful, whereas foreign elements, especially of Arab origin, are impure and destructive." (99) Indeed, according to Akhavân, the Arabs are devils, literally "Ahriman," the force of darkness and evil:

> Though now the European corruption
> Playing a thousand tricks, makes frequent incursions,
> The Arab filth and disgrace is more repulsive
> More corruptive is this old woe.
> Whatever praiseworthy, good and beautiful
> Whatever pure and Ahuric
> This old [Arab] Ahriman has plundered and still he doth
> Has killed, swallowed up, and still he doth. (100)

According to Akhavân, the Arabs have corrupted every aspect of Iranian culture, from religion, myth and legend to language, literature, and history:

> Indeed, one does not talk of the licentious, unrestrained Mazdak that the shameless, lying Arab has introduced to us by his historians and flatterers; and not the Zoroaster, the Buddha, and the Mâni that have been presented to us wrongly, through lies; but the wise, noble, high-minded Mazdak, the seeker of equality.... (101)

> The inauspicious Arab traditions and the horrible and defiling ailments of Arabization have contaminated our traditional poetry not only in respect to form, metre, rhyme, and rhetorical system, but most of the poetic works and our national language Fârsi (Persian) have also been, for their mythical background, under the domination of Semitic [and] Arabic [and] Islamic legends. (brackets added) (102)

In fact, Akhavân sees the role of modernist poet as having great cultural and historical significance:

> Most of the forms of our poetry as well are derived from the Arabs, for example qasideh, qet'eh, and so on, although in this also some differences can naturally be found, but in our new poetry we have gotten closer to the free indigenous forms, especially the pre-Islamic forms. (103)

It is worth noting that Akhavân's quarrel is with "Semitic *and* Arabic *and* Islamic legends." (emphasis added) (104) In his discussion of "non-Iranian" influences on traditional Persian literature, he refers again to "Arab and Semitic stories", and "non-Iranian, Semitic and Islamic stories" (105). His quarrel is not with Islamic influence alone, but with Semitic influence as well, as he makes clear:

> It may occur to someone that a legend is a legend and what difference does it make whether the source of the legend is in the Torah [Old Testament], in the Gospels, or in the *Avestâ* and the *Khudây-Nâmeh*? Yes this is true;... [but] today, to compensate for past negligence, we could do justice to a grand world of beauty and felicity... a grand and wondrous, forgotten world, that of the legendary heritage of our own Aryan ancestors. (106)

Thus Akhavân sets "Iranian and Aryan legends" (107), the "heritage of our own Aryan ancestors," against the Semitic influences on Iranian culture. In so doing he is again like Hedâyat, in that he sees Iranians and Arabs as two different and unequal races, one Aryan and superior, the other Semitic and inferior, and blames the Muslim Arab invaders for destroying Iran's true, Zoroastrian cultural identity. In Akhavân's view, the Iranian Self was pure, bright and beautiful, but has been corrupted by the Arab Other, false, dark, and evil.

Nâder Nâderpour (b. 1929)

The poet Nâder Nâderpour has not wished to break with the classical Persian literary tradition, but to update it, developing forms and content appropriate to modern times. (108) While Nâderpour's poetry is praised for its imagery and language, it has been often criticized as well, up to the late 1970s, for its lack of social and political *engagement*. (109) However, poems written after the establishment of the Islamic Republic of Iran in the spring of 1979, and particularly after Nâderpour's subsequent emigration to Paris in 1980, are modernist in form and explicitly social and political in content, a change seemingly forced by his opposition to the Islamic Republic of Iran. Nâderpour was not active in the movement against the Pahlavi regime, and unlike many secular intellectuals who had come to support Khomayni, "he was never for a moment inclined to support the Khomayni movement because he was aware from the beginning, as he puts it, of Khomayni's true character" (110). It is his belief that "the Khomayni revolution has had essential, permanent, and assuredly negative consequences for Iranian culture." (111) According to Michael Hillmann:

> Nâderpour has always had strong feelings about Shi'ism and the Shi'i clergy, viewing internal Iranian political history from the beginning of the century as a rightful attempt to reduce the influence of Shi'i clerics in Iranian society. The specific achievements of the Constitutional Movement (1905-1922) in Nâderpour's view were twofold: the development of a sense of nationalism and the introduction of *laïcité* into Iranian life. Nâderpour views Twelver Shi'i Islam in general as Islam's most superstitious and insidious manifestation with its special days of mourning, ritual self-flagellation, saint worship, and the like. For that matter, in Nâderpour's view, the Iranian population in the last days of the Sasanian Era (224-640s) misunderstood Islam in seeing it

as a salvation from imperial oppression and other problems:
thirsting for a Mazdakite society of equality and brotherhood,
Iranians were deceived into thinking that Islam represented
such values. (112)

Nâderpour rejects Islam, not from the existentialist position of
some other writers (113) but from the position of a secular nationalist
who sees Islam as alien and fundamentally opposed to true Persian
Iranian culture and values. Not only does Nâderpour see Islam as
inimical to Persian Iranian nationalism and *laïcité*, he argues that there
is a contradiction between "l'âme iranienne et l'esprit islamique":

> Bien sûr, l'Islam, comme toute religion, ne
> connaissant ni nationalité ni frontière, est internationale.
> Elle dépasse toutes ces limites afin de réaliser sa vocation,
> sinon son ambition universaliste. Pourtant l'Islam, plus
> qu'aucune autre religion, appartient à un peuple, le peuple
> arabe, et à une terre, l'Arabie. Son prophète, son livre sacré et
> sa langue rituelle témoignent tous de cette appartenance. Or
> cette religion, malgré son internationalisme prononcé, est
> devenue par la suite l'un des piliers les plus sûrs du
> antinationalisme arabe. Elle ne s'oppose guère aux
> nombreuses nationalités—apparemment divergentes, mais
> profondément unies—de son peuple.
>
> Pour l'Iran cependant, la situation est différente. Le
> peuple iranian, avec ses origines, son ancienne religion et sa
> langue indo-européenne, n'aurait sans doute pas adhéré à
> l'Islam si les événements historiques n'avaient pas réussi à
> captiver son âme, car ce peuple avait, lui aussi, son
> nationalisme. Une analyse approfondie de ces éléments nous
> conduit à cette conclusion que la littérature persane, dès sa
> renaissance, après la conquête arabe et jusqu'à nos jours,
> malgré ses apparences islamiques n'est qu'un symbole du
> perpétuel conflit entre l'esprit de cette religion et l'âme
> iranienne et que toutes les révoltes, successives et
> contradictoires, ne sont que l'envers en l'endroit d'une seule
> médaille: la pénitence d'un péché. (114)

Nâderpour's poetry reflects his opposition to Islam as antithetical to
Iranianness as well.

In "Khotbeh-ye Bahâri" [Springtime Declaration] (1978) (115),
Nâderpour recasts traditional Jewish, Christian, and Islamic imagery, to
empty it of that meaning and transform it into the Persian cultural
motif of *noruz*, the beginning of the new year in the spring. Spring,
rather than Jesus, is the "messiah,"

whose miraculous hand
made living creatures jealous of dead plant life,
who cured the thin, sick sapling,
who rejuvenated the old earthbound tree....

Spring is the "season's prophet" as well, the "fresh harbinger of Mt.
Sinai" which replaces God's prophet, Moses:

You, who with one breeze can cause the fire of oranges
to burn and grow from a green branch,
with the command of the staff entrusted to you
make a split in the heart of the night's indigo waves
so that you might lead the migration of the sun's tribe.

Here the imagery is positive, with the "sun's tribe" referring to Iranians
as a people with their traditional solar calendar; it is an image which
recurs in other poems as well, although less happily.

Lest one be misled by the seeming neutrality of the religious
imagery transformed in "Springtime Declaration," Nâderpour's famous
poem "Qom" (1954) makes clear his antipathy toward Islam. The city
which is Shi'i Iran's theological center is portrayed as lifeless, stagnant,
decaying:

Thousands of women
thousands of men
the women in scarfs
the men in cloaks
a single gold dome
with old storks
a joyless garden
with a few scattered trees
devoid of laughter
silent
a half-filled courtyard pool
with greenish water
some old crows
on piles of rocks
crowds of beggars
every step of the way
white turbans
black faces (116)

"Qom" is anti-Islamic without being anti-Arab; anti-Islamic
sentiments do not have to be anti-Arab. But Nâderpour's antipathy is
not only toward Islam, but toward Arabs as well. In "Shâm-e

Bâzpasin" [The Last Supper] (1978), written before the establishment of the Islamic Republic, Nâderpour's image of Arabs evokes pre-Islamic Arab ignorance:

> Like desert-roaming Arabs,
> we dug the graves of virtuous girls
> in the salt desert of ignorance and madness. (117)

In poems written after the establishment of the Islamic Republic, however, the perceived enmity between Persian Iranianness and Arab Islam is made even more explicit. In "Tolu'i az Maghreb" [A Sunrise from the West] (1982), Iran is the "birthplace of Mithraic sun and love," the "showcase of the fire of Zoroaster," the "kingdom without dusk," the "ancient nest of the phoenix," where now

> after the dawn of blood, there is no sign of the sun:
> a red moonlight from the eastern horizon
> shines on the burned faces
> and imitates the lost sun. (118)

Here the lunar culture of Arab Islam has invaded, overturning the solar civilization of Iran and setting things awash in blood.

The same image of Arabs as savage, alien intruders who destroy traditional Iranian civilization is repeated in "Injâ va Ânjâ" [Here and There] (1986), but here the darkness is complete; even the moon has vanished:

> From afar I see my own land drenched in blood
> and the expiration of the sun in its sky.
> There, after the migration of spring
> and the flight of the moon,
> only winter exists and boundless night.
> There, if no news rises
> from the well spring of animals,
> in its darkness are signs of beastly habits.
> The glow that shines in men's eyes
> is wilder than the gleam in the look of animals.
> There, the race of the millers of history
> has on its face the brand of ruinous shame.
> There, 'Omar is perpetually victorious
> over ill-fated Yazdgerd.
> There, for millennia, the rapacious, pitiless desert
> is intoxicated with imbibing blood.
> Whoever brings the name of the sun to his lips
> is a fire-worshipper in the eyes of those Bedouins.

There, women in the tents of desert dwellers
do not believe the sun except in thought.
However much giving birth is their ancient custom,
out of fear of adding to the horde of martyrs
they no longer desire to be mothers.
There, in accordance with Arab custom,
the lash has no qualms about incursion
on the back of the intoxicated.
The judge can turn criminals upside down
from the mountains into the boundless desert. (119)

Nâderpour compares the establishment of the Islamic Republic to the conquest of the Sâsânid empire by the Muslim Arabs in the 7th century, and suggests that it is in fact a continuation of that same defeat of Iranian culture at the hands of bloodthirsty Arabs. In Nâderpour's view, Islamic tenets are "Arab custom," and Muslim Iranians are now ignorant and intolerant Bedouins. He suggests that perhaps it is this same Arab ignorance and intolerance which has driven away even the moon.

The poems are as much anti-Arab as anti-Islamic, because Nâderpour sees Islam both as wrong in itself, and wrong because it is Arab. In his view, Arabs are dark, savage and inhuman, their culture epitomized by images of the irrational, blood and the moon. Islam may be appropriate to Arabs, but not to Iranians, whose enlightened civilization finds expression in images of Zoroastrian fire, the sun and springtime. According to Nâderpour, to be a Muslim, or a supporter of the Islamic Republic of Iran, is to be Arab and therefore not Iranian, indeed therefore almost less than human. Like that of Hedâyat, Chubak and Akhavân-e Sâles, his is a racist argument.

Notes

1. Michael Craig Hillmann, "Introduction to 'Persian is Sugar'," *Major Voices in Contemporary Persian Literature*, edited by Michael Craig Hillmann, *Literature East and West* 20 (1980): 11.
2. Mohammad Ali Jamâlzâdeh, "Fârsi Shekar Ast" [Persian is Sugar], *Yeki Bud Yeki Nabud* [Once Upon a Time], fifth printing (Tehrân: Sharq, 1954), pp. 22-37; translated by Seyed Manoochehr Moosavi, *Major Voices*, pp. 13-20.
3. Maxime Rodinson, *The Arabs*, translated by Arthur Goldhammer (Chicago: University of Chicago Press, 1981), p. 45.

4. Hassan Kamshad, *Modern Persian Prose Literature* (Cambridge: Cambridge University Press, 1966), pp. 108-109.

5. Ibid., p. 91.

6. Mohammad Ali Jamâlzâdeh, *Sar o Tah-e Yek Karbâs* [Cut from the Same Cloth] (Tehrân: Kânun-e Ma'rifat, 1956); translated by W. L. Heston, *Isfahan is Half the World: Memories of a Persian Boyhood* (Princeton, NJ: Princeton University Press, 1983), p. 57.

7. Ibid., p. 17.

8. Ibid., p. 51.

9. Ibid., p. 237.

10. Ibid., p. 171.

11. Kamshad, *Modern Persian Prose Literature*, p. 110.

12. Mohammad Ali Jamâlzâdeh, Preface to *Yeki Bud Yeki Nabud* [Once Upon a Time], fifth printing (Tehrân: Sharq, 1954), pp. 5-21; translated by Haideh Daragahi, "The Shaping of the Modern Persian Short Story: Jamalzadih's 'Preface' to *Yiki Bud, Yiki Nabud*," *The Literary Review* 18 (Fall 1974): 25.

13. Ibid., pp. 25, 27.

14. Sâdeq Hedâyat, *Alaviyeh Khânom*, fourth printing (Tehrân: Amir Kabir, 1963), pp. 9-57; translated by Gisele Kapuscinski and Mahin Hambly, "The Pilgrimage," *Sadeq Hedayat: An Anthology*, edited by Ehsan Yarshater (Boulder, CO: Westview Press, 1979), pp. 1-39.

15. Sâdeq Hedâyat, "Talab-e Âmorzesh" [Seeking Forgiveness], *Seh Qatreh Khun* [Three Drops of Blood], sixth printing (Tehrân: Amir Kabir, 1962), pp. 73-88; translation mine. Also translated by Brian Spooner, "The Search for Mercy," *Sadeq Hedayat: An Anthology*, pp. 53-62; and by Minoo S. Southgate, "Seeking Absolution," *Iranian Studies* 9 (1976): 49-59.

16. Sâdeq Hedâyat, "Sag-e Velgard" [The Stray Dog], *Sag-e Velgard*, seventh printing (Tehrân: Amir Kabir, 1963), pp. 9-22; translated by Brian Spooner, *Sadeq Hedayat: An Anthology*, pp.119-126.

17. Kamshad, *Modern Persian Prose Literature*, pp. 108-109.

18. Sâdeq Hedâyat, "Abji Khânom," *Zendeh be Gur* [Buried Alive], sixth printing (Tehrân: Amir Kabir, 1963), pp. 73-84; translated by Siavosh Danesh, "The Spinster," *Sadeq Hedayat: An Anthology*, pp. 1-40.

19.. Sâdeq Hedâyat, *Buf-e Kur* [The Blind Owl] fourteenth printing (Tehrân: Amir Kabir, 1973); translated by D. P. Costello (New York: Grove Press, 1969).

20. Ibid., p. 52.

21. Ibid., p. 91.

22. Ibid., p. 53.

23. Ibid., p. 107.

24. Ibid., p. 109.

25. Elton Daniel, "History as a Theme of *The Blind Owl*," *Hedâyat's 'The Blind Owl' Forty Years After*, edited by Michael Craig Hillmann (Austin, TX: The University of Texas at Austin Center for Middle Eastern Studies, Middle East Monographs No. 4, 1978), p. 82.

26. Hedâyat, *The Blind Owl*, p. 61.

27. Ibid, p. 56.

28. Sâdeq Hedâyat, "Dâsh Âkol," *Seh Qatreh Khun* [Three Drops of Blood], sixth printing (Tehrân: Amir Kabir, 1962), pp. 43-62; translated by Richard Arndt and Mansur Ekhtiar, *Sadeq Hedayat: An Anthology*, pp. 41-52.

29. Mâshâllâh Âjoudâni, "Hedâyat va Nâsyonâlism" [Hedâyat and Nationalism], *Irânnâmeh* 10, No. 3 (Summer 1992), p. 7. See also Homa Katouzian, *Sâdeq Hedâyat: The Life and Literature of an Iranian Writer* (London and New York: Taurus, 1991).

30 Sâdeq Hedâyat, "Sâyeh-ye Moghul" [The Mongol's Shadow], *Anirân* [Non-Iranian], *Majmu'eh Neveshtehâ-ye Parâkandeh Sâdeq Hedâyat* [A Collection of the Scattered Works of Sâdeq Hedâyat], second printing (Tehrân: Amir Kabir, 1965), pp. 102-118; translated by D. A. Shojai, *Chicago Review* 20 (1969): 95-104.

31. Sâdeq Hedâyat, "Zendeh be Gur" [Buried Alive], *Zendeh be Gur*, sixth printing (Tehrân: Amir Kabir, 1963), pp. 9-38; translated by Brian Spooner, *Sadeq Hedayat: An Anthology*, pp. 145-162.

32. Sâdeq Hedâyat, *Hâji Âqâ* (Tehrân: Jâvidân, 1977); translated by G. M. Wickens (Austin, TX: The University of Texas at Austin Center for Middle Eastern Studies, Middle East Monographs No. 6, 1979), p. 45.

33. Sâdeq Hedâyat, "Esfahân Nesf-e Jahân" [Esfahan is Half the World], *Parvin Dokhtar-e Sâsân va Esfahân Nesf-e Jahân* [Parvin the Sâsânid Girl and Esfahan is Half the World], third printing (Tehrân: Amir Kabir, 1963), pp. 57-118; translation mine, pp. 89-90.

34. Sâdeq Hedâyat, *Tarâneh'hâ-ye Khayyâm* [Songs of Khayyâm] (Tehrân: Mosavvar, 1963), p. 40; cited by Leonard Bogle, "The Khayyâmic Influence in *The Blind Owl*," *Hedâyat's 'The Blind Owl' Forty Years After*, p. 89.

35. Ehsan Yarshater, "Introduction," *Sadeq Hedayat: An Anthology*, pp. vii-xiv.

36. Carter Bryant, "Hedâyat's Psychoanalysis of a Nation," *Hedâyat's 'The Blind Owl' Forty Years After*, p. 161.

37. Sâdeq Hedâyat, *Parvin Dokhtar-e Sâsân* [Parvin the Sâsânid Girl], third edition (Tehrân: Amir Kabir, 1963), pp. 8-56; translation mine.

38. Ibid., p. 15.

39. Ibid., pp. 20-21.

40. Ibid., p. 20.

41. Ibid., p. 50.

42. Ibid., p. 13.

43. Ibid., pp. 15-32.

44. Ibid., p. 37.

45. Ibid., pp. 21-23.

46. Ibid., p. 21.

47. Ibid., pp. 22-23.

48. Ibid., p. 38.

49. Ibid., p. 10.

50. Ibid., p. 38.
51. Ibid., p. 10.
52. Ibid., p. 10.
53. Ibid., p. 46.
54. Ibid., pp. 46-47.
55. Ibid., p. 47.
56. Ibid., pp. 46-47.
57. Âjoudâni, "Hedâyat and Nationalism," p. 7.
58. Michael Craig Hillmann, "Introductory Note," *Major Voices*, pp. 71-72.
59. Sâdeq Chubak, "Cherâgh-e Âkhar" [The Last Offering], *Cherâgh-e Âkhar* (Tehrân: M. H. Elmi, 1966), pp. 9-74; translation mine.
60. Sâdeq Chubak, *Tangsir*, third printing (Tehrân: Jâvidân, 1973); translation mine.
61. Sâdeq Chubak, "Monsieur Elias," *Kheymeh-shab-bâzi* [The Puppet Show], fifth printing (Tehrân: Jâvidân, 1975), pp. 179-198; translation mine.
62. Sâdeq Chubak, "Ba'd az Zohr-e Âkhar-e Pâ'iz" [An Afternoon in Late Autumn], *Kheymeh-shab-bâzi* [The Puppet Show], fifth printing (Tehrân: Jâvidân, 1975), pp. 199-220; translated by Carter Bryant, *Iranian Studies* 15 (1982): 69-79.
63. Sâdeq Chubak, *Sang-e Sabur* [The Patient Stone], third printing (Tehrân: Jâvidân, 1976); translated by M. R. Ghanoonparvar, "Sâdeq Chubak's *The Patient Stone*: A Translation and Critical Introduction," (Ph.D. dissertation, The University of Texas at Austin, 1979); published as Sâdeq Chubak, *The Patient Stone*, translated by M. R. Ghanoonparvar (Costa Mesa, CA: Mazdâ, 1989). References are to the published work.
64. M. R. Ghanoonparvar, "Introduction," *The Patient Stone* by Sâdeq Chubak, translated by M. R. Ghanoonparvar (Costa Mesa, CA: Mazdâ, 1989), p. xii.
65. Ibid., p. xx.
66. Chubak, *The Patient Stone*, p. 19.
67. Ibid, p. 4.
68. Ibid., p. 2.
69. Ibid., p. 37-38.
70. Ibid., pp. 48-50.
71. Ibid., pp. 96.
72. Ibid., p. 85.
73. Ibid., p. 146.
74. Ibid., pp. 33.
75. Ibid., pp. 94-96.
76. Ibid., pp. 17.
77. Ghanoonparvar, "Sâdeq Chubak's *The Patient Stone*," p. 131.
78. Chubak, *The Patient Stone*, p. 130-131.
79. Ibid., pp. 149.
80. Ibid., pp. 150.
81. Ibid., p. 21.

82. Ibid., p. 101.
83. Ibid., pp. 133.
84. Ibid., pp. 143-144.
85. Ibid., pp. 62-73.
86. Ibid., p. 62.
87. Ibid., pp. 33.
88. Ghanoonparvar, "Sâdeq Chubak's *The Patient Stone*," p. 125.
89. Ibid., p. 125.
90. Chubak, *The Patient Stone*, p. 153.
91. Ibid., p. 169.
92. Mehdi Akhavân-e Sâles, *Arghanun* [The Organ], second printing (Tehrân: Morvârid, 1969), p. 126; cited by Sorour S. Soroudi, "The Iranian Heritage in the Eyes of the Contemporary Poet Mihdi Akhavan Salis (M. Omid)," *Towards A Modern Iran*, edited by Elie Kedourie and Sylvia G. Haim (London and Totowa, NJ: Frank Cass and Co., 1980), p. 135.
93. M. R. Ghanoonparvar, *Prophets of Doom: Literature as a Socio-Political Phenomenon in Modern Iran* (Lanham, MD: University Press of America, 1984), p. 15.
94. Mehdi Akhavân-e Sâles, "Âkhar-e *Shâhnâmeh*" [The Ending of the Shahnameh], *Âkhar-e Shâhnâmeh* [The Ending of the Shahnameh], third printing (Tehrân: Morvârid, 1989), pp. 79-86; translated by Sorour Soroudi, "Akhavan's 'The Ending of Shahnameh': A Critique," *Iranian Studies* 2 (1969): 80-96; and by Michael Craig Hillmann, *Iranian Culture: A Persianist View* (Lanham, MD: University Press of America, 1990), pp. 16-18.
95. Michael Craig Hillmann, *Iranian Culture: A Persianist View* (Lanham, MD: University Press of America, 1990), p. 18.
96. Mehdi Akhavân-e Sâles, "Shush râ Didam" [I Saw Susa], *Ferdowsi* 24, No. 1098 (December 1972): 13; translated by Leonardo P. Alishan, "Trends in Modernist Persian Poetry" (Ph.D. dissertation, The University of Texas at Austin, 1982), pp. 64-66; also "Seven Poems (1955-1972) by Mehdi Akhavân-e Sâles," *Major Voices*, pp. 141-143.
97. Soroudi, "The Iranian Heritage," p. 133.
98. Mehdi Akhavân-e Sâles, Epilogue to *Az in Avestâ* [From This Avestâ] (Tehrân: Morvârid, 1965), pp. 109-222; cited by Soroudi, "The Iranian Heritage," p. 138.
99. Soroudi, "The Iranian Heritage," p. 135.
100. Akhavân-e Sâles, *From This Avestâ*, p. 222; cited by Sorour S. Soroudi, "Myth and Legend as a Key to Reality and VIsion in the Works of Mihdi Akhavan Salis (M. Omid)," *Asian and African Studies* 12 (1978): 376.
101. Akhavân-e Sâles, *From This Avestâ*, pp. 153-154; cited by Soroudi, "The Iranian Heritage," pp. 138-139.
102. Akhavân-e Sâles, *From This Avestâ*, p. 214; cited by Soroudi, "Myth and Legend," p. 369.
103. Akhavân-e Sâles, *From This Avestâ*, p. 208; translation mine.

104. Akhavân-e Sâles, *From This Avestâ*, p. 214; cited by Soroudi, "Myth and Legend," p. 369.

105. Akhavân-e Sâles, *From This Avestâ*, pp. 214-215; translation mine.

106. Akhavân-e Sâles, *From This Avestâ*, pp. 215-216; cited by Soroudi, "Myth and Legend," p. 370.

107. Akhavân-e Sâles, *From This Avestâ*, p. 215; translation mine.

108. Alishan, "Trends in Modernist Persian Poetry," pp. 161-166; Ghanoonparvar, *Prophets of Doom*, p. 119; Michael Craig Hillmann, "Nâder Nâderpour and Thirty Years of Persian Poetry," Introduction to *False Dawn: Persian Poems by Nâder Nâderpour*, translated by Michael Craig Hillmann, *Literature East and West* 22 (1986), pp. 8-9.

109. Ghanoonparvar, *Prophets of Doom*, p. 81; Hillmann, "Nâder Nâderpour and Thirty Years of Persian Poetry," p. 17.

110. Hillmann, "Nâder Nâderpour and Thirty Years of Persian Poetry," p. 25.

111. Ibid., p. 27.

112. Ibid., p. 5.

113. Alishan, "Trends in Modernist Persian Poetry," pp. 170-173.

114. Nâder Nâderpour, "Une contradiction: l'âme iranienne et l'esprit islamique," *Die Welt des Islams* 23-24 (1984): 134-135.

115. Nâder Nâderpour, "Khotbeh-ye Bahâri" [Springtime Declaration], *Az Âsmân tâ Rismân* [From the Sublime to the Ridiculous] (Tehrân: Morvârid, 1978), pp. 53-55; translated by Hillmann, *False Dawn*, pp. 56-57.

116. Nâder Nâderpour, "Qom," *Chashmhâ va Dasthâ* [Eyes and Hands] (Tehrân: Safi 'Alishâh, 1954), pp. 169-170; translated by Hillmann, *False Dawn*, p. 34.

117. Nâder Nâderpour, "Shâm-e Bâzpasin" [The Last Supper], *Shâm-e Bâzpasin* (Tehrân: Morvârid, 1978), pp. 76-82; translated by Hillmann, *False Dawn*, pp. 61-63.

118. Nâder Nâderpour, "Tolu'i az Maghreb" [A Sunrise from the West], *Sobh-e Dorughin* [False Dawn] (Paris: Nehzat-e Moqâvemat-e Melli-ye Irân, 1982), pp. 127-131; translated by Hillmann, *False Dawn*, pp. 69-71.

119. Nâder Nâderpour, "Injâ va Ânja" [Here and There], handwritten text supplied by the poet to Michael Craig Hillmann; translated by Hillmann, *False Dawn*, pp. 76-79.

Chapter 3

Women's Writings,
Women's Views

Chapter 3 looks at writings by three women: the poets Forugh Farrokhzâd (1934/35-1967) and Tâhereh Saffârzâdeh (b. 1936), and short story writer and novelist Simin Dâneshvar (b. 1921). Except for a few poems by Saffârzâdeh, the works discussed were written before 1979 and the establishment of the Islamic Republic of Iran. While the views of the three women differ greatly from those of the men in Chapter 2, they differ as well among themselves. Chapter 5 discusses the significance of these differences.

Forugh Farrokhzâd (1934/35-1967)

Forugh Farrokhzâd's poetry does not reflect concern with the issues of history, national(ist) politics, or even culture in the same way as the writings of many of her male peers. It was not that she lived in circumstances unaffected by government policies—she was born in 1934/35 in Tehrân, and with her father in the military, her family was part of the new middle class. She also lived in Ahvâz for three years, and visited Khuzestân again to work on film projects. Khuzestân's population is, of course, overwhelmingly Arab. Farrokhzâd was also a modern, anti-establishment intellectual. Yet there are no images of Arabs in any of her poems.

Farrokhzâd married in 1952, when she was sixteen, and as her husband was employed in the Finance Ministry in Ahvâz, she moved there and lived with him there until 1955. During that time she wrote the poems collected in *Asir* [The Captive] (1955). Yet these poems in general "lack an explicit Islamic environment or palpable Iranian settings."(1) Images specific to Ahvâz appear in only two of the poems. In "Yâdi az Gozashteh" [A Remembrance of the Past], Farrokhzâd describes a lover in Ahvâz, city of the Kârun river with groves of date palms along its banks:

> It is a city by that clamoring river
> with date palms interlaced and nights full of light. (2)

In "Anduh" [Sorrow], a lover is remembered through a description of night along the river:

> On the waters of the river, the shadows of the date palms
> tremble in the sensuous breeze of midnight. (3)

Aside from the lover and the speaker, there are no other people, Persian or Arab, in the poems. Interestingly enough, Farrokhzâd does use the Arabic *shatt* instead of the more common Persian *rud(khâneh)* to refer to the river; given the efforts of the Pahlavi regime to change the Arabic name of the nearby Shatt al-Arab to the Persian name Arvand Rud, the word *shatt* would hold for some people political connotations. While the images of the Kârun and palms establish the setting in Khuzestân, there is no reference to Khuzestân's Arabs.

Among the poems in *Divâr* [The Wall] (1956), the Kârun river appears in two more poems, in "Teshneh" [Thirsty] (4) as the name of the river along whose banks grows the flower speaking in the poem, and in "Shekufeh-ye Anduh" [Blossom of Sorrow]:

> At nights near the palm groves
> the Kârun cries of its suffering
> as if my cries of regret
> are heard by the tired waves. (5)

One wonders why there are no more images recognizable as part of life in Ahvâz. Perhaps the personal, introspective nature of the poems themselves precludes much attention to the external world. Perhaps even that external world was such that the Arab character of the region did not much impinge upon the consciousness of Farrokhzâd or other Persians living in Khuzestân. For during the 1950s many Iranians immigrated to Ahvâz from outside of Khuzestân; in 1956, officially, only 54 percent of the population of Ahvâz had been born in Khuzestân.(6) Furthermore, even in 1976, there was little integration of Persian and Arabs, and even various trades and professions tended to be dominated by certain groups—for example, retail trades and crafts by people from Esfahân, public baths and stone masonry by people from Khuzestân. (7) Thus Farrokhzâd might have had little interaction with Arabs in Ahvâz.

In 1959, Farrokhzâd edited a film about an oil well fire near Ahvâz, photographed by Shâhrokh Golestân, and she went to Khuzestân herself to work on films, one of which, *Water and Heat* (1961), "portrayed the dizzying social and industrial 'heat' of the Âbâdân environment."(8) Again, Farrokhzâd might not have seen the Arabs there. In 1956, in Abadan, 42 percent of blue-collar workers, 26 percent of white-collar workers, and 9 percent of managers were from Khuzestân. The rest were from Fârs and Esfahân, in the case of blue-collar workers, and increasingly from Tehrân and the north-western provinces, in the case of white-collar workers and management. (9) The social and industrial environment, in other words, was predominantly Persian, and even the Árabs that were a part of it would not have been easily identified as such, since they would have had to know Persian, and to wear Western clothes or uniforms.

Farrokhzâd's poems do not address the issue of Iranianness, and all the historical, cultural, social and political implications thereof. Farrokhzâd could find little that applied to her in what were essentially masculine history or politics; according to Michael Hillmann, "she did not have the time to engage dillettantishly in the world of public and exclusively male politics. Hers was a more serious, elemental political struggle for her own identity."(10)

Only in a couple of Farrokhzâd's poems is there any sense of historicity, and indeed the sense which is present is hardly conventional. In "Ma'shuq-e Man" [My Beloved] (1964), the speaker describes her beloved as one

> whom I
> in this ominous, strange land
> have hidden like the last trace
>   of a great religion
> in the thicket of my breasts. (11)

The image is suggestively historical, but could be understood in the same way as the images of "Âyeh-hâ-ye Zamini" [Earthly Verses]" (1964) as images of apocalypse:

> What bitter and black days.
> Bread had conquered
> the wonderful power of prophecy.
> Hungry and impoverished prophets
> fled from God's promised lands. (12)

Farrokhzâd's social or political poems derive from her experiences in Tehrân. Poems like " O Jewel-Studded Land," "To Ali His Mother Said One Day," "Someone Who Is Not Like Anyone," and "I Feel Sorry for the Garden" are perhaps best appreciated "as a symbolic rejection of prevailing attitudes."(13) Those poems which deal more specifically with the oppression of women still work along the same lines, like "Wedding Band," "Friday," and "The Windup Doll." Two rather more generalized poems—"Call to Arms" and "To My Sister"—were never included by Farrokhzâd in any collections of her own verse.(14)

Some of these social poems are clearly critical of the institution of Islam. Farrokhzâd herself had concluded that "Allâh did not exist, and that afterlife in the form of Islamic heaven is a myth."(15) In "Arusak-e Kuki" [The Windup Doll] (1964), Islam is one of the deadening choices offered to women:

> One can genuflect a whole lifetime
> with bowed head at the foot
>   of a saint's cold sarcophagus.
> One can find God in a nameless grave.
> One can find faith with an insignificant coin.
> One can rot in the precincts of a mosque
> like an old prayer reader. (16)

And in "Delam Barâye Bâgh Misuzad" [I Feel Sorry for the Garden] (1966), one of the people responsible for the garden's demise is Mother, whose

> whole life
> is a prayer rug spread
> at the threshold of fear or hell.
> At the bottom of everything Mother always
> searches for traces of sin
> and thinks that a plant's *kofr*
> has contaminated the garden. (17)

But while Islam is criticized, it is criticized as an Iranian, not as an alien or Arab, institution.   In "I Feel Sorry for the Garden," the father is also to blame:

> And from dawn to dusk in his room
> he reads either the *Shâhnâmeh*
> or *Nasekh ol-Tavârikh.*

While the mother cares only for religion, the father cares only for national history; both are equally reprehensible.

In fact, from *'Esyân* [Rebellion] (1958) on, Islamic imagery appears in a number of Farrokhzâd's poems (18), and such imagery is often positive, as in "Kasi Keh Mesl-e Hichkas Nist" [Someone Who Is Not Like Anyone] (1966):

> And his name just like Mother
> says it at the beginning
>   and at the end of prayers
> is either 'judge of judges'
> or 'need of needs'.
> And he can do something
>   so that the neon Allâh sign
> which was as green as dawn
> will shine again
> in the sky above the Meftahiyân Mosque.(19)

Farrokhzâd uses the term *âyeh*, which denotes a verse from the Quran, in both "Earthly Verses" and "Tavallodi Digar" [Another Birth], but with very different implications.   In the first, in contrast to the words of heaven, the verses are the words of the earth and utter depravity; in the second, the image is wholly affirming:

> My whole being is a dark chant
> that perpetuating you
> will carry you to the dawn
>   of eternal growths and blossomings.(20)

Here, Farrokhzâd "intended by the term to communicate an impression of something indestructible, such as the words of Allâh as recorded in Koranic verses." (21) She does not, however, imply belief in Islam in using the term.

Farrokhzâd sought to affirm her identity, a part of which is her Iranianness, in her dedication to her individuality in life and in poetry.

"Fath-e Bâgh" [Conquest of the Garden] (1962) is such a statement of affirmation:

> Everyone is afraid,
> everyone is afraid, but you and I
> joined with the lamp and water and mirror
> and we were not afraid.
> Everyone knows,
> everyone knows
> we have found our way
>   into the cold, quiet dreams of the phoenixes;
> we found truth in the garden....(22)

According to Hillmann, hers is a positive, feminine Iranianness which refuses to accept Iranian patriarchy and so, like Sohrâb, offers Iran a more positive model. (23)

Unlike the previous writers, Farrokhzâd's anti-Islamic sentiments are not anti-Arab; anti-Islamic sentiments do not have to be anti-Arab. Moreover, Farrokhzâd refuses to participate in the same kind of nationalist discourse. Unlike the men, she has no need to establish an historical identity as an Iranian; nor does she need to establish her cultural identity as an Iranian at the expense of another. Farrokhzâd does not need the Arab Other to define her Self.

Tâhereh Saffârzâdeh (b. 1937)

A very different point of view is that of the poet Tâhereh Saffârzâdeh, who spent 1968-69 in the United States studying to receive a Master of Fine Arts degree, and wrote and published poems in English during that period. (24) According to Leonardo Alishan, Saffârzâdeh's writing career shows an increasing concern with the "search for self" and the "quest for spiritual-religious identity vis-à-vis the harsh realities of modern society" (25), and her answer to both has been a return to Islam. Because Saffârzâdeh is a practicing Muslim, she approaches the question of Arabs and Iranians from a different perspective. In Saffârzâdeh's view, Islam is a universal, not an Arab, phenomenon. Her world view is not nationalist, but rather Islamic and universalist.

Moreover, Saffârzâdeh's understanding of Islam requires not only personal but also social morality: "[My renewed attraction to Shi'ism] has as its source my own basic love of justice and my hatred of oppression and compromise. The philosophy of Shi'ism has for its basis and for its power of motivation the love of justice and it is strongly opposed to compromise." (26)

So Saffârzâdeh's poetry deals not only with personal concerns but with larger, social concerns, not only in Iran but wherever they may appear in the world. Thus, in "Az Ma'bar-e Sukut va Shekanjeh: Taqdim beh Artesh-e Jomhurikhâh-e Irland" [Through the Passageway of Silence and Torture: dedicated to the Irish Republican Army] (1987), written as "a lament for Bobby Sands," she declares that,

> the cry of the wounded seeking justice
> finds refuge
> not in the courts of men
> but in the rivers,
> in the Shannon and Kârun,
> in the Ganges and Mekong.
> Your way and ours, and the way of the people of Palestine,
> the way of all oppressed peoples,
> are connected to each other
> by the path of torture,
> by the path of silence and domination. (27)

In "Sepidi-ye Sedâ-ye Siâh" [The Whiteness of the Black's Voice] (1987), she refers to Johannesburg (28); in "Az Shikâgo" [From Chicago] (1971), she refers to "a Guernica not in Spain." (29)

In "Safar-e Avval" [The First Journey] (1970), Saffârzâdeh alludes to Hindu funeral pyres, and reflects on the Hindi word "âchâ":

> You pronounce "âchâ" so beautifully,
> âchâ
> âchâ
> âchâ
> it is a strange word
> it has an expansive music with a depressed echo
> let's look at the word separate from its music .... (30)

As Leonardo Alishan explains, "âchâ" means "yes," "whatever you command." In short, as Saffârzâdeh later explained, "despite the beautiful sound inherent in "âchâ," it is, when semantically observed, the symbol of 'Eastern servitude'." (31)

But unlike Hedâyat, who in *The Blind Owl* drew a spiritual closeness between India and Iran, Saffârzâdeh turns to Islam, and Arabia. And instead of the Hindi of "The First Journey," or Hedâyat's Sanskrit, the reader now hears another, more powerful, language, the Arabic of the Quran, venerated as the language of revelation and Islam. In "Safar-e Âsheqâneh" [The Love Journey] (1977), Saffârzâdeh quotes Surah 111:1, "The power of Abu Lahab will perish, and he will perish":

"Tabbat yada abi Lahaben wa tabb"
"Tabbat yada abi Lahaben wa tabb"
"Tabbat yada abi Lahaben wa tabb"
And this sound
which is beyond the potential of a human voice
finds its way into my veins. (32)

In the same way, the *azân*, call to prayer, is an important motif.
"Fath Kâmel Nist" [Victory is not Complete] (1970) begins:

The pure sound of the azân is heard.
The pure sound of the azân
is like the believing hands of a man
who plucks from my healthy roots
the feeling of growing distant, getting lost,
        becoming an island,
and I walk towards a great prayer .... (33)

The azân is heard again in "Safar-e Salmân" [Salmân's Journey] (1977):

The pure sound of the azân is heard
the good voice of Balâl
and he walks towards a great prayer
and all of us walk with him
with Salmân
in the courtyard
a courtyard of equality and justice. (34)

While in the first poem, the conquest had not been completed because
of "the bread's cruelty," in "Salmân's Journey" the conquest is complete
because that cruelty has been resolved in "a courtyard of equality and
justice." (35)

One finds Arabs as well as Arabic in her poetry. In "Through
the Passageway of Silence and Torture," Saffârzâdeh refers to the people
of Palestine (36); and in "Deltangi" [Homesickness] (1971), to the
Egyptian soldiers killed in battle against Israel:

Our brothers die in Sinai,
There is no tomb for them—
the orchards of the Nile Valley have been rented out. (37)

They are not called Arabs; their Arabness is not denied, but it is not
important. Indeed, Saffârzâdeh is concerned with them not as Arabs,
but as another oppressed people, like the people of Ireland or Iran, or in
the case of "our brothers in Sinai," as fellow Muslims, brothers in

Islam. Hers is a very different consciousness from that of the men writers previously discussed. When other Arab characters appear, what is important is that the figures are Islamic, rather than Arab.

In "The Love Journey," Saffârzâdeh refers through Surah 111 to Abu Lahab, the prophet Muhammad's uncle and bitter opponent. (38) In "Safar-e Zamzam" [The Zamzam Journey] (1970), the speaker of the poem, a woman on a pilgrimage undertaken in search of faith rather than as a result of it, addresses the guide of the pilgrims, the Prophet Mohammad's uncle Abu Tâleb, in what becomes a refrain: "Hold the bridle firmly, Abu Tâleb." (39) What matters about him in terms of this poem is not his Arabness, but the fact that, while he protected Mohammad against the enemies of Islam, he never became a Muslim. He is someone who has not found faith, like the speaker until the end of the poem, when she says that she will disobey the guide and say, "Oh God, do not turn away from me."

This is not to say that Saffârzâdeh denies her own Persian Iranian history or identity. But her nationalism is very different from that of Hedâyat, Akhavân-e Sâles or Nâderpour. In "Khamposhtân" [The Stooping Ones] (1987), Saffârzâdeh laments the degradation of Iran at the hands of "the stooping ones," and turns to another Islamic figure, Khalil (the Prophet Abraham) who bowed not to idols but to God alone, as one whose example should be followed:

> This ancient plateau
> this great and high plateau of yesterday
> today, oh alas,
> is a tired and forsaken pit
> in which is thrown
> the rubbish of the foreigners.
> Khalil was the first enemy of the stooping men. (40)

And in "The Love Journey," she refers to the Islamic figures of Joseph and Job as she again bewails the sad state of Iran:

> "Tabbat yada abi Lahaben wa tabb"
> "Tabbat yada abi Lahaben wa tabb"
> "Tabbat yada abi Lahaben wa tabb"
> And this sound
> which is beyond the potential of a human voice
> finds its way into my veins.
> One has to keep on the way.
> In vain I am staying
> and staring at the Baluch
> who for the sake of amusement
> eats grass three times a day

and prays three times a day.
And my love is for a captive land
With Joseph's face
And Job's patience.
Mândâneh was a shepherd's mother
and the mother of causes.
The night of the martyrdom of Persian flowers
Oh you lovers of Persian calligraphy, poetry and language,
Mândâneh was witness that
you were men of feasts and idleness,
men of feasts and festivals. (41)

Saffârzâdeh's Iranianness brings together Persian Iranian elements, other Iranian elements, and Islamic elements. She alludes to Mândâneh, mother of Cyrus the Great, and Persian calligraphy, poetry and language, and to the Baluchi tribal and village people of southeastern Iran, a recognition of Iran's ethnic diversity. She also invokes Islamic elements: Joseph, Job, and the Quran, and finds the solution to Iran's degradation in the words of the Quran: to cut off the hands of Abu Lahab, to fight against Western imperialism as the enemy of Iran and Islam.

Saffârzâdeh directly addresses the question of Iranianness and Islam in "Safar-e Salmân" [Salmân's Journey] (42), the story of Salmân the Persian, and a particularly relevant text, as Alishan suggests:

> The significance of "Salmân's Journey" is two-fold. Firstly, in the context of modernist Persian poetry, it is the first major poem by a prominent Persian poet, which portrays the Arab invasion of the Sasanian Iran not as a tragedy but as a salvation. It is also the first poem where the religion of Islam is portrayed as a means for deliverance from economic inequality and political tyranny. When compared with a poem like Mehdi Akhavân-e Sâles' "Âkhar-e Shâhnâmeh" [The Ending of the *Shâhnâmeh*] in which the poet compares the contemporary anguish of Iran to the time when the empire fell to the Arabs, "Salmân's Journey" reveals not only the extent of its poet's unorthodox and fresh world-view, but it also becomes a prophetic foretelling of what Iran has undergone in the course of the revolution of 1978-79 and beyond. (43)

Salmân is popularly known as the first Persian to embrace Islam. Saffârzâdeh portrays him as "the awake Persian," disturbed by the corruption and injustice of Sâsânid society:

Why are the peasants
dear in the *Yashthâ*
and low in the royal courtyard
kissing feet
worthless
on the thin crops of wheat
on the soft stems of plants
the heavy dust of taxation
the weight of taxation
the expense of smiles and jesters
the expense of tipping the best dancers
the heavy expense of fortune tellers
why expensive fortune tellers
good thoughts come from us
good deeds come from us
the good world goes to the king
why the good world
          for the king....

Salmân sets out to find truth:

Going leads to the road
staying, to stagnation
Salmân went on the road
with loving feet
and the road joined him ....

He finds no answers with the Zoroastrians, Jews or Christians:

Perhaps the green spring
will answer his call
but, like the synagogue and the temple,
the walls of the church held no answer.

Salmân leaves Sâsânid Iran for Arabia, where he finds the prophet
Mohammad and becomes a Muslim and Companion of the Prophet:

His hand was loosed from the palm branch
His hand was delivered to the root
and his hand
was joined
to the strong root,
to the true faith.
The pure sound of the azân is heard
the good voice of Balâl
and the qiblahs of events

> along the direction of time
> had answered his prayers.
> And he had entered the circle of truth,
> and his entrance was the entrance of us all.

Salmân returns with the Muslim army, the "army of truth," to Iran:

> They were not Arabs
> they were not Persians
> they were citizens of the kingdom of Truth
> they were liberating
> they were liberation.
> Men of clamoring blood,
> men of tumult and storm
> on naked horses,
> who, with the loving hands of Faith,
> chanting "Allâh, Allâh,"
> take their lives as gifts
> into the battlefield.

Saffârzâdeh sees the invaders not as Arabs conquering Iran, but as Muslims bringing the liberating truth of Islam to a people waiting to embrace it:

> The walled cities, waiting and sorrowful,
> the cities awaiting the blessing of attack,
> one by one
> are opened and submit [to Islam] ....

There are none of Hedâyat's images of violation. In Saffârzâdeh's view, the Iranians welcome the Arabs, and their conquest of Iran is really liberation.

With the victory of Islam, Salmân returns to lead the people's prayer:

> The pure sound of the azân is heard
> the good voice of Balâl
> and he walks towards a great prayer
> and all of us walk with him
> with Salmân
> in the courtyard
> a courtyard of equality and justice.

This is the image of the Golden Age, but unlike the writers discussed earlier, who hearken back to Iran's pre-Islamic past, Saffârzâdeh sets the

Golden Age both outside Iran at the time of the Prophet and in Iran with the advent of Islam.

Two points need to be emphasized. First, Salmân is important to Saffârzâdeh not just an individual, but as the exemplar of all Persian Muslims: "And he had entered the circle of truth / and his entrance was the entrance of us all." Even the poem's arrangement, in two sections, underlines the necessity of both personal and social responsibility: in the first section Salmân finds faith, and in the second, he returns to Iran to share his faith with others. Secondly, Saffârzâdeh emphasizes the essential universalism of Islam in her description of the Muslim army: They were not Arabs / they were not Persians / they were citizens of the kingdom of Truth." Thus, even as Salmân is the prototype of Persian Muslims, his national identity underscores Islamic universalism: "his face had the dust of travel / his face, the color of searching."

It is that same universality of Islam that Saffârzâdeh addresses in "Sepidi-ye Sedâ-ye Siâh" [The Whiteness of the Black's Voice] (1987):

> The pure sound of azân is heard,
> the good sound of Balâl.
> The sound of that Ethiopian,
> that black,
> dips, like a thunderbolt,
> over the roof of idolatry and ignorance
> After "there is no God"
> the affirmation, "but God."
> "God is great" is heard from all directions.
> Balâl
> has come near the prophet.
> Also near him has come
> Sohayb, unexpectedly, from Rome,
> Salmân
> has arrived from Persia,
> so that the isolation of color
> would result in one color. (44)

Just as Salmân is the prototype of converted Persians, Balâl represents the Africans, and Sohayb the Europeans, and it is their becoming "one color" in Islam which Saffârzâdeh offers as the solution to the present-day "age of the barbarism of the sons of science."

Saffârzâdeh's nationalism is anti-Western imperialist rather than anti-Arab. Hers is the Islamic political model, instead of the Western; instead of a national or racial confrontation between Iranians and Arabs, Saffârzâdeh sees an ideological confrontation with Western imperialism and materialism. There are Arabs in her poems, but no Arab Other, and the nationality of her characters is important only insofar as it points up the internationalist character of Islam. Although Saffârzâdeh does not deny her Iranianness, she writes as a Muslim first, and as an Iranian second. Her Iranian identity is important nonetheless, in that her nationality, her language, culture, and history, provide the specific context within which she practices her Islam. But even here her Iranianness is on a smaller, more personal, scale; in acknowledging a multi-ethnic Iran, her identity as a Persian Iranian is just one of many possibilities.

Simin Dâneshvar (b. 1921)

Simin Dâneshvar's treatment of Arabs is part of her very different definition of Iranianness. Dâneshvar's novel *Savushun* (1969), the best selling novel in the history of modern Persian literature (45), communicates a vision of Iran which embraces people of different ethnic groups within the framework of a shared Iranian culture, where pre-Islamic Iranian elements join with Islam to produce a complementary whole.

Dâneshvar hails from Shirâz, the capital of Fârs province, home of the Qashqâ'i and Boyer Ahmadi tribespeople who appear in *Savushun*. Like Saffârzâdeh, Dâneshvar is aware of ethnic differences, and she recognizes them in her work as neutral fact, as one more point of description. For example, in *Savushun*, she refers to a "Turkoman driver." (46) The tribespeople appear as real people, some sympathetic, some less so, rather than characters reduced to an ethnic stereotype.

The same recognition is found in "Tasâdof" [The Accident] (1959) (47), where Nâdereh/Nadia, the wife of the narrator, is "a gift from Ahvâz"; she tells her husband how, when she passed the exam for her driver's license, "the examining officer was so pleased that he complimented her: 'Madame, you have stored up all of our southern sun,' because my wife has a very dark complexion." Although Nâdereh is not identified as an Arab, Dâneshvar's description of her recognizes that people from Khuzestân are ethnically different from other people in Iran.

In *Savushun*, however, Dâneshvar refers explicitly to the Arabs of Khuzestân. Khânom Fâtemeh wants to go to Karbalâ:

> I'll take a suitcase and get myself to Ahvâz. The rest is easy.
> I'll walk my way through the palm groves. I'll find the Arabs;
> I'll give each a gold dinar; they'll put me on a boat and take
> me across the river. Then I'll be free. I'll be neither

oppressor nor oppressed. It won't be my country, and I won't
be so heartbroken. (48)

Khânom Fâtemeh could as easily have said, "I'll find the date farmers."
Instead, she recognizes the Arabs as Arabs.

There is one other reference to Arabs in the novel, when Khânom
Fâtemeh tells Zari about her mother's flight to Karbalâ.

> We never did find out how Bibi got to Karbalâ, but we heard
> that when she got there, she fell into the clutches of Skaykh
> Abbas Qomi. Shaykh Abbas wore a long gown to look like
> an Arab and scared the pilgrims with threats that he would
> report them and do this, that, or the other. (49)

Here, what looks like an Arab cleric turns out to be an unscrupulous
Persian. Shaykh Abbas is an interesting counterpart to the mullah of
Jamâlzâdeh's "Persian is as Sweet as Sugar". In Jamâlzâdeh's story, the
Iranian mullah turns out to be not only ridiculous but also, in
Ramazân's eyes, not "really" Iranian either, but "really" an Arab and a
demon. Here we have the reverse.

In "Keyd al-Khâ'enin" [Traitor's Intrigue] (1959) (50),
Dâneshvar's Âqâ again brings to mind Jamâlzâdeh's mullah. While the
story ostensibly concerns a retired colonel, the Âqâ stands at the center
of the story. All the events of the story lead back to the other
characters' relations to him; he is like a compass needle around which
all the other characters and events turn. The story of the colonel's
change of heart is the story of the colonel's changed relationship with
the Âqâ, expressed through the colonel's struggle to greet the Âqâ and to
have the Âqâ return his greeting.

The reader first sees the Âqâ sitting in the cold street. He is
poor, virtuous and devout:

> Right across the mosque sat a man with a brown cloak and
> cap. A brazier of burning coal was in front of him and he was
> reciting the Quran.... He had a pale face with almost colorless
> eyes; his lips had even less color. His cloak and tunic were
> old, but clean.

His coloring is remarkable. While one might expect him to have a pale
complexion, since he is not a laborer, his eyes and lips are colorless as
well, as if Dâneshvar has removed any racial characteristics to
underscore the universalist character of the Âqâ as a Muslim. At the
same time, the language of his recitation is Arabic, and, as in

Jamâlzâdeh's story, the issue of Arabic is of central importance. Indeed, the title of the story is Arabic.

The Âqâ had been the prayer leader at the mosque, and had preached there as well, but has been banned from both, following his arrest for anti-government statements:

> He was preaching from the pulpit, 'People of Islam, all this blood shed in the cause of truth has not been wasted.... The noble Quran has been my mentor. So I announce: Hail to Abraham, whose purpose was to build, and may the two hands of Abi Lahab be cut off, as he was a hypocrite and a coward.' Of course, he was there reciting verses in Arabic and interpreting them, and how the crowd was moved!

As in the first description of the Âqâ, there is again a seeming contradiction here between the universalism of Islam, seen in the the the Âqâ's appeal to the People of Islam, and the Arabic language of the Quran; Arabic is a foreign language to most Iranians. Certainly the Âqâ's Arabic infuriates the colonel: at their next meeting, "the colonel involuntarily said hello. The man didn't reply; he looked up and said something in Arabic, of which the colonel understood only the word 'traitors'." When the colonel refuses to apologize, "the cloaked man threw out a verse in Arabic. The colonel went home and sat in the sitting room in a filthy mood. Well done, thanks a lot. A measly mullah doesn't respond to one's salutation, curses in Arabic which one can't even understand." When his wife asks him what is wrong, he answers:

> "I said hello to a mullah across from the Asadi mosque and he totally ignored me. The day Keyvan's pigeon died, he insulted me and the boy in front of everyone. Today he cursed me in Arabic. Why the hell should he be allowed to curse in a language I don't understand?"

The people listening to the Âqâ's sermon, however, have no problem with the Arabic parts, and Arabic is a problem to the colonel only while he is still angry with the Âqâ.

For the colonel's point of view begins subtly to change, as the reader learns that he has worked for thirty years, but was never promoted beyond the rank of colonel. His wife wears a *châdor*, and had stopped attending receptions with her husband many years ago, because of the gambling and alcohol, and the fact that the others made fun of her. The focus of the colonel's anger begins to change, and the reader begins to see that it is not just the colonel against the Âqâ, it is the government against Islam:

> "You are taking out your frustrations on me," answered Mansureh Khânom quietly, "But I'm not going to argue with you now. Remember, I'm not your foe. We have put up with each other for thirty years. Don't worry if the Âqâ hasn't responded to your greeting. Say hello a second, a third, even a tenth time. It's the likes of you that have caused him all this misfortune."
>
> "Woman, this man is opposing the government," said the colonel. "I, on the other hand, earn my living from the government. You expect me to go and kiss his hand? Say hello to him again? Not in a hundred years. Let him dream on."
>
> "You will because you're not an evil man at heart," said Mansureh Khânom. "Be assured the Âqâ divides all the Islamic taxes between the families of the poor. His own family lives modestly on a flat-woven carpet."
>
> "Why is he demeaning himself? Why? Why is he sitting across from the mosque in this bitter cold weather? Is there nowhere else to go? Why doesn't he just sit in his own home?"
>
> "He's probably got the endurance," said Mansureh Khânom. "In his heart he knows he's right. He has faith."

So, when the colonel drives his wife to the Âqâ's house to deliver food, the colonel's reaction to Arabic is neutral, rather than angry:

> The Âqâ's house was old. Above the front door was a mosaic with Arabic script on it. The colonel took his glasses from his pocket and stepped out of the car. He put the glasses on and read the verse of the mosaic, "Nasr min Allah wa fath ghareeb—Victory comes from God, and victory is near." It was cold. He returned to the car.

Finally, on his way home from shopping, the colonel sees two men beating and dragging away the Âqâ, and two other men struggling to free him. It is an epiphany for the colonel:

> The colonel came closer and turned to the two men. "What do you think you're doing? What business do you have with the Âqâ?"
>
> And all of a sudden it slipped out: "Aren't you Muslims?"

And when he is suddenly afraid for what he has said, still he goes on.

> He had to take a risk. Whatever would be, would be. There weren't many years left for him or for his wife. His wife had longed for it; it was she who insisted, time and again, that one should be either a true Muslim or no Muslim at all.

The colonel has changed sides, and can finally exchange greetings with the Âqâ. He helps the Âqâ into his car, brings his cloak and hat, and drives to his house, where the Âqâ can have some tea:

> The colonel was in bliss. Laughing, he said, "Excuse me, I forgot to greet you."
> The Âqâ said, "Assalâm-u aley-kom va Rahmatollâh va Barakato—Peace be upon thee, and the mercy of God and His blessing."

The plot has revolved around the issue of the colonel's greeting and being greeted by the Âqâ. The resolution of the plot, the Âqâ's greeting to the colonel, is in Arabic. But Arabic is clearly not a foreign language in the context of Islam. Dâneshvar suggests that the Arabic of the Quran is not a foreign language to Muslim Iranians.

Dâneshvar's vision of Iran in *Savushun* includes people of different ethnic groups with a shared Iranian mythology of common meaning but different forms, for example, pre-Islamic Iranian mythology in the mourning for Siyâvash, and Iranian Shi'i Islam in the mourning for Imam Hosayn. Indeed, it is from the Turkish-speaking Qashqâ'i tribesmen, the brothers Malek Rostam Khân and Malek Sohrâb, that Zari learns the story of Siyâvash, in their tent, where "all around ... were painted images of Rostam, Ashkabus, Esfandiyâr, and Sohrâb." (51) The ceremony of mourning for Siyâvash called *savushun*, has already been intermingled with Islamic elements:

> But the sun hasn't come up yet when that dear one appears on the mountain riding his horse. He looks as if he is saying his prayers while he is riding. He puts a Quran on his head and prays for all Muslims. 'Almighty God.'
> The dervish takes the reins of the rider's horse and says, 'Take a sip in the memory of the thirsty lips of Hosayn.'"(52)

Throughout the novel, the stories of Siyâvash and Hosayn run parallel to each other. With Yusef's death, the imagery of each becomes interchangeable: Zari weeps for Siyâvash; Khânom Fâtemeh wants to make a Karbalâ of Shirâz; seeing Fâtemeh, Zari is reminded of Her Holiness Zaynab. When the funeral procession passes Yusef's mare, "She neighed twice. It seemed as if tears flowed out of the mare's eyes onto her nose; her nostrils flared. Zari remembered what the middle aged woman had said years ago about the story of Savushun." (53) When the police stop the funeral procession, one of the mourners tells the captain:

> "We are mourning our fellow townsman. Suppose this is Karbalâ and today is Âshurâ. You wouldn't want to be a Shemr, would you?"
> Someone invoked, "Yâ Hosayn." And the crowd replied in a drawn-out chant, "Yâ Hosayn!"
> Or suppose it is Savushun and we are mourning Siyâvash, Zari thought bitterly. (54)

Dâneshvar sees the same meaning, differently encoded, in the stories of Siyâvash and Hosayn.

Indeed, Dâneshvar sees both pre-Islamic Iranian culture and Islam as Iranian. Dâneshvar allows for much difference among Iranians, but sees an essential unity at the level of belief in myth and religion. This produces a cultural synthesis which, for Dâneshvar, is essentially Iranian. While Jamâlzâdeh, unlike Hedâyat, Chubak, Akhavân-e Sâles and Nâderpour, accepts Islam, he still sets an Iranian Self against an Arab Other. For Dâneshvar, however, both Islamic and Arab elements in Iranian culture have an Iranian, rather than a foreign character.

Like Saffârzâdeh, Dâneshvar accepts ethnic diversity; there are Arabs, and others, but there is no Arab Other. Dâneshvar is concerned with social justice as well, and, like Saffârzâdeh again, in "Traitors' Intrigue" and *Savushun*, the Other is Western imperialism and its manifestations in Iran, the Pahlavi regime and British occupation troops during World War II. Hers is a more humanistic view, and very different from the views of Hedâyat, Chubak, Akhavân-e Sâles and Nâderpour.

Notes

1. Michael Craig Hillmann, *A Lonely Woman: Forugh Farrokhzâd (1935-1967) and Her Poetry* (Washington, DC: Mage Publishers and Three Continents Press, 1987), p. 16.

2. Forugh Farrokhzâd, "Yâdi az Gozashteh" [A Remembrance of the Past], *Asir* [The Captive], seventh printing (Tehrân: Amir Kabir, 1972), pp. 47-49; translation mine.

3. Forugh Farrokhzâd, "Anduh" [Sorrow], *Asir* [The Captive], seventh printing (Tehrân: Amir Kabir, 1972), pp. 151-153; translation mine.

4. Forugh Farrokhzâd, "Teshneh" [Thirsty], *Divâr* [The Wall], sixth printing (Tehrân: Amir Kabir, 1975), pp. 137-142.

5. Forugh Farrokhzâd, "Shekufeh-ye Anduh" [Blossom of Sorrow], *Divâr* [The Wall], sixth printing (Tehrân: Amir Kabir, 1975), pp. 107-112; translation mine.

6. *Encyclopedia Iranica*, Volume 1, edited by Ehsan Yar-Shater (London, Boston and Henley: Routledge and Kegan Paul, 1985), s.v. "Ahvâz," by X. de Planhol, pp. 688-691.

7. Ibid.

8. Hillmann, *A Lonely Woman*, pp. 42-43.

9. *Encyclopedia Iranica*, Volume 1, edited by Ehsan Yar-Shater (London, Boston and Henley: Routledge and Kegan Paul, 1985), s.v. "Âbâdân" by X. de Planhol, pp. 51-57.

10. Hillmann, *A Lonely Woman*, p. 46.

11. Forugh Farrokhzâd, "Ma'shuq-e Man" [My Beloved], *Tavallodi Digar* [Another Birth] (Tehrân: Amir Kabir, 1964), pp. 78-82; translated by Hillmann, *A Lonely Woman*, p. 41.

12. Forugh Farrokhzâd, "Âyeh-hâ-ye Zamini" [Earthly Verses], *Tavallodi Digar* [Another Birth] (Tehrân: Amir Kabir, 1964), pp. 97-105; translated by Hillmann, *A Lonely Woman*, pp. 48-51.

13. Hillmann, *A Lonely Woman*, p. 47.

14. Ibid., p. 95.

15. Forugh Farrokhzâd, as quoted in an interview with Sadroddin Elâhi, *Immortal Forugh Farrokhzâd*; cited by Hillmann, *A Lonely Woman*, p. 92.

16. Forugh Farrokhzâd, "Arusak-e Kuki" [The Windup Doll], *Tavallodi Digar* [Another Birth] (Tehrân: Amir Kabir, 1964), pp. 71-75; translated by Hillmann, *A Lonely Woman*, pp. 81-83.

17. Forugh Farrokhzâd, "Delam Barâye Bâgh Misuzad" [I Feel Sorry for the Garden], *Imân Biyâvarim beh Âghâz-e Fasl-e Sard* [Let Us Believe in the Beginning of the Cold Season] (Tehrân: Morvârid, 1973), pp. 45-54; translated by Hillmann, *A Lonely Woman*, pp. 119-122.

18. Hillmann, *A Lonely Woman*, p. 34.

19. Forugh Farrokhzâd, "Kasi Keh Mesl-e Hichkas Nist" [Someone Who Is Not Like Anyone], *Imân Biyâvarim beh Aghâz-e Fasl-e Sard* [Let Us

Believe in the Beginning of the Cold Season] (Tehrân: Morvârid, 1973), pp. 58-66; translated by Hillmann, *A Lonely Woman*, pp. 65-68.

20.   Forugh Farrokhzâd, "Tavallodi Digar" [Another Birth], *Tavallodi Digar* [Another Birth] (Tehrân: Amir Kabir, 1964), pp. 164-169; translated by Forugh Farrokhzâd and Karim Emami, in Hillmann, *A Lonely Woman*, pp. 111-113.

21.   Hillmann, *A Lonely Woman*, p. 113.

22.   Forugh Farrokhzâd, "Fath-e Bâgh" [Conquest of the Garden], *Tavallodi Digar* [Another Birth] (Tehrân: Amir Kabir, 1964), pp. 125-129; translated by Hillmann, *A Lonely Woman*, pp. 96-97.

23.   Hillmann, *A Lonely Woman*, pp. 90-91.

24.   Leonardo P. Alishan, "Trends in Modernist Persian Poetry" (Ph.D. dissertation, The University of Texas at Austin, 1982), p. 254.

25.   Alishan, "Trends in Modernist Persian Poetry," p. 253.

26.   Tâhereh Saffârzâdeh, "Goft-e gu bâ Mohammad 'Ali Esfahâni" [Interview with Mohammad Ali Esfahâni], *Harakat va Diruz* [Movement and Yesterday] (Tehrân: Ravâq, 1978), p. 162; cited by Alishan, "Trends in Modernist Persian Poetry," p. 267; a revised version of Alishan's chapter on Tâhereh Saffârzâdeh appeared as "Tâhereh Saffârzâdeh: From the Wasteland to the Imam," *Iranian Studies* 15 (1982): 181-210.

27.   Tâhereh Saffârzâdeh, "Az Ma'bar-e Sukut va Shekanjeh: Taqdim beh Artesh-e Jomhurikhâh-e Irland" [By the Path of Silence and Torture: Dedicated to the Irish Republican Army], *Didâr-e Sobh* [Meeting the Morning] (Shirâz: Navid, 1987), pp. 24-34; translation mine.

28.   Tâhereh Saffârzâdeh, "Sepidi-ye Sedâ-ye Siâh" [The Whiteness of the Black's Voice], *Didâr-e Sobh* [Meeting the Morning] (Shirâz: Navid, 1987), pp. 157-160.

29.   Tâhereh Saffârzâdeh, "Az Shikâgo" [From Chicago], *Sadd va Bâzuân* [The Dam and the Arms] (Tehrân: Zamân, 1971), pp. 34-36.

30.   Tâhereh Saffârzâdeh, "Safar-e Avval" [The First Journey], *Tanin dar Deltâ* [Echo in the Delta] (Tehrân: Amir Kabir, 1970), pp. 4-30; translated by Alishan, "Trends in Modernist Persian Poetry," p. 262.

31.   Alishan, "Trends in Modernist Persian Poetry," p. 262.

32.   Tâhereh Saffârzâdeh, "Safar-e Âsheqâneh" [The Love Journey], *Safar-e Panjom* [The Fifth Journey] (Tehrân: Ravâq, 1977), pp. 61-90; translation mine.

33.   Tâhereh Saffârzâdeh, "Fath Kâmel Nist" [Victory is not Complete], *Tanin dar Deltâ* [Echo in the Delta] (Tehrân: Amir Kabir, 1970), pp. 94-96; translation mine.

34.   Tâhereh Saffârzâdeh, "Safar-e Salmân" [Salmân's Journey], *Safar-e Panjom* [The Fifth Journey] (Tehrân: Ravâq, 1977), pp. 9-44; translation mine.

35.   Alishan, "Trends in Modernist Persian Poetry," pp. 266-267.

36.   Saffârzâdeh, "By the Path of Silence and Torture," *Meeting the Morning*, pp. 24-34.

37. Tâhereh Saffârzâdeh, "Deltangi" [Homesickness], *Sadd va Bâzuân* [The Dam and the Arms] (Tehrân: Zamân, 1971), pp. 25-27; translation mine.

38. Saffârzâdeh, "The Love Journey," *The Fifth Journey*, pp. 61-90.

39. Tâhereh Saffârzâdeh, "Safar-e Zamzam" [The Zamzam Journey], *Tanin dar Deltâ* [Echo in the Delta] (Tehrân: Amir Kabir, 1970), pp. 32-47.

40. Tâhereh Saffârzâdeh, "Khamposhtân" [The Stooping Ones], *Mardân-e Monhani* [The Crooked Men] (Shirâz: Navid, 1987); in Tâhereh Saffârzâdeh, *Selected Poems*, translated and edited by M. H. Kamyabee and N. Mirkiani (Shirâz: Navid, 1987), pp. 111-113.

41. Saffârzâdeh, "The Love Journey," *The Fifth Journey*, pp. 61-90; translation mine.

42. Saffârzâdeh, "Salmân's Journey," *The Fifth Journey*, pp. 9-44; translation mine.

43. Alishan, "Trends in Modernist Persian Poetry," p. 264.

44. Saffârzâdeh, "The Whiteness of the Black's Voice," *Meeting the Morning*, pp. 157-160; translation mione.

45. Farzaneh Milani, "Power, Prudence, and Print: Censorship and Simin Daneshvar," *Iranian Studies* 18 (1985): 328.

46. Simin Dâneshvar, *Savushun*, sixth printing (Tehrân: Khârazmi, 1974); translated by M. R. Ghanoonparvar (Washington, DC: Mage Publishers, 1990), p. 259.

47. Simin Dâneshvar, "Tasâdof" [The Accident], *Beh Ki Salâm Konam?* [To Whom Should I Say Hello?], third printing (Tehrân: Khârazmi, 1984), pp. 53-74; translated by Maryam Mafi, *Dâneshvar's Playhouse* (Washington, DC: Mage Publishers, 1989), pp. 31-52.

48. Dâneshvar, *Savushun*, p. 89.

49. Dâneshvar, *Savushun*, p. 107.

50. Simin Dâneshvar, "Keyd al-Khâ'enin" [Traitors' Intrigue], *Beh Ki Salâm Konam* [To Whom Should I Say Hello?], third edition (Tehrân: Khârazmi, 1984), pp. 239-266; translated by Maryam Mafi, *Dâneshvar's Playhouse*, pp. 85-112.

51. Dâneshvar, *Savushun*, p. 65.

52. Ibid., pp. 339-340.

53. Ibid., p. 368.

54. Ibid., p. 371.

Chapter 4

A Man in the Middle

Having seen the ends of the spectrum of images of Arabs, attention now turns to the views of one writer in the middle of that spectrum, Jalâl Âl-e Ahmad (1923-1969). Âl-e Ahmad was a major author of fiction and non-fiction, and the most important social critic in Iran from the late 1950s until his death. Âl-e Ahmad wrote to make readers aware of the problems he saw facing Iran, and wrote as well in search of answers. He traces Iranian social problems to a number of causes, which are some of Âl-e Ahmad's most persistent themes: political and cultural nationalism, defining Iranianness, the clash between religious and secular outlooks and values, and the impact of modernization and the West on Iran.

Even more important, however, is Âl-e Ahmad's sympathy towards Islam. Indeed, as Michael Hillmann points out, "Even without his many literary achievements, Âl-e Ahmad would remain particularly significant and controversial in Iran today because of his assumption that Twelver Shi'i Islam is a necessary core component of Iranianness and because of an alleged inclination on his part toward a religious government." (1) Thus, an analysis of the images of Arabs in Âl-e Ahmad's works was chosen as the fairest and most revealing analysis of works by a prominent writer, defender of Persian Iranian cultural nationalism and sympathetic to Islam as well, a man caught in the middle.

Jalâl Âl-e Ahmad (1923-1969)

Like Hedâyat, Jalâl Âl-e Ahmad was deeply concerned with Iranianness, its definition and its defense. However, while Hedâyat had argued for an Iranianness based on pre-Islamic "Aryan" cultural identity, and so rejected Islam as an alien "Semitic" presence, Âl-e Ahmad does not reject Islam, even if his own belief is problematic. Rather, Âl-e Ahmad's criteria for Iranianness are the Persian language, Persian Iranian culture, and Shi'i Islam.(2)

Âl-e Ahmad offers this definition of Iranianness fully aware of the existence of non-Persian peoples in Iran. In *Gharbzadegi* [Plagued by the West] (1962) he refers to the coup which brought Rezâ Shâh Pahlavi to power, and the following "forced settlement of the Kurds, the suppression of "Semitqu" [a Kurdish leader], and the elimination of Shaykh Khaz'al [Shaykh of Mohammerah, or Khorramshahr, in Khuzestân] who, had he behaved a bit more intelligently, could have become like one of the Shaykhs of the Persian Gulf Emirates." (3) Indeed, three of Âl-e Ahmad's closest associates and fellow writers were Gholamhosayn Sâ'edi (1935/36-1985), Samad Behrangi (1939-1968), and Rezâ Barâheni (b. 1935), Turks from Âzarbâyjân, who would not have agreed with Âl-e Ahmad's view of the Persian language as an essential element in defining Iranianness. (4) Barâheni writes:

> The Shah considers all Iranians to be Aryans, thus overlooking the ethnic diversity which exists in the country. Everyone has to learn one language, Persian. This is a great injustice to the other nationalities.
>
> I belong to the Turkish-speaking Azarbaijani nationality. The men and women of my generation were told by the Shah to forget about their language and to read and write everything in Persian. We did so under duress and learned Persian. When I write a poem or a story about my parents, my mother, who is alive and doesn't know how to read or write or speak Persian, cannot understand it. I have to translate it for her so that she can understand.
>
> The Shah's efforts to Persianize the Azarbaijanis and the Kurds and the Arabs and the Baluchis have failed. But his cultural discrimination still prevails. For instance, the 3,000 American children brought to Iran by their parents working for Grumman can go to an English-speaking school. Yet millions of native Iranian children born to Azarbaijani, Kurdish and Arab parents do not have even one school in which they can study everything in their native languages. This is only one aspect of the Shah's racism. (5)

Interesting in this regard is Âl-e Ahmad's commemorative essay "Samad va Afsâneh-ye 'Avâm" [Samad and the Folk Legend] (6), written for Samad Behrangi in 1968. Samad was a teacher and educational reformer, the author of *Kand o Kâv dar Masâ'el-e Tarbiyati-ye Irân* [An Investigation of Educational Problems in Iran] (1965), and of other essays on education, as well as short stories, children's stories, translations of Âzarbâyjâni Turkish folk tales into Persian, and essays on Âzarbâyjân. Âl-e Ahmad had admired Samad and his work. In his essay, Âl-e Ahmad refers to him as "this younger brother."

> Once he came with one of his stories and with his folkloric poem inscribed as a dedication on the first page.... Which made me realize how romantic he was and, at the same time, how insistent he was in revitalizing his mother tongue— meaning, beware of the presence of this separating sickle which is Aras along with other bisecting elements—whose presence we have not tolerated in our schools and culture for the past fifty or sixty years. Another time he was at a party where two or three university professors were present. Because of Samad's presence, the discussion shifted towards the Turkish language, which made me realize how bold he was, how fiery, and how sharp. I had thought that only I had these qualities!

Âl-e Ahmad apparently recognizes and sympathizes with Âzarbâyjâni cultural nationalism. On the other hand, his references to "this wakeful conscience of an exiled culture," and his reference again to the Aras river as "this separating sickle, this bisector of one culture and one language" could just as easily be motivated by Iranian nationalist outrage at the loss of half of Âzarbâyjân to Czarist Russia with the treaty of Torkmanchai in 1828.

Âl-e Ahmad was hardly alone in facing the contradictions inherent in working out an Iranian cultural identity. Many culturally nationalistic Persian Iranian intellectuals face a real dilemma, insofar as they see Islam as the religion of the Arab invaders of the seventh century, and a modern, secular world view as essentially Western. (7)

Âl-e Ahmad struggled with this dilemma, most notably in *Plagued by the West* and *Lost in the Crowd* (8), and in his explicit recognition of the problem, and in his coming down on the side of Shi'i Islam as something essential to Iranianness, Âl-e Ahmad differed from most contemporary writers. Âl-e Ahmad's special significance lay in his recognition of traditional Shi'i Islam as the world view of most Iranians, and in his recognition of the potential Shi'i Islam held as a social and political force in Iran. (9) The majority of Iranians live in a culturally Islamic, if not Shi'i, milieu, even if they themselves are not practicing (Shi'i) Muslims, and Âl-e Ahmad recognized that, if not for Shi'i Islam, there is no other most common denominator in Iran, given its great differences in geography, language, regional customs and cultures. There is no other cultural factor so widely shared.

But while Âl-e Ahmad values religious morality, he condemns superstition and legalism. Many of Âl-e Ahmad's short stories are critical of traditional religious beliefs and practices. In "Gonâh" [The Sin] (1949), where a young girl feels guilty for having fallen asleep on her father's bed, Âl-e Ahmad deals with traditional attitudes toward women, and the barely-suppressed sexual hysteria arising therefrom. (10) In "Seh'târ" (1949), where a perfume-seller smashes a musician's instrument in front of the mosque, Âl-e Ahmad presents religion as opposed to art, music, and individuality. (11) Yet other stories, while criticizing religious traditions, affirm religious morality by presenting religious characters in a positive way.

In "Eftâr-e Bimowqe" [The Untimely Breaking of the Fast] (1945), Amiz Rezâ, a Tehrân bazaar broker, travels to Qazvin by bus in order to be able to break his fast and drink tea during Ramazân, on the authority of the Âqâ, the local cleric. Âl-e Ahmad condemns the legalism and superstition of Shi'i Islam, and the willingness of Amiz Rezâ to allow the Âqâ to think for him. Yet, while Amiz Rezâ is stupid, he is also hard working and honest: "He was a religious man who had never been content, like some of his compatriots during these last few tumultuous years, to wheel and deal and secure his fortune." (12)

A more positive presentation of a religious character is found in "Ziyârat" [The Pilgrimage] (1945) (13), a short story describing Âl-e Ahmad's pilgrimage to Karbalâ in 1943:

> I had made friends with a middle-aged man sitting beside me. He was a grocer by trade and he told me his story. He had a family of five to support and until two years ago was drawing a miserable wage from his master who had a shop in the Qazvin caravanserai. The day came when he could bear it no longer. One evening in the mosque he broke down in front of the entire congregation and prayed to God to deliver him from the dog's life he was living, before he became too old: to get him away somewhere where he could have a house of his own however small, set up a little shop of his own perhaps, and have enough left over from his own needs to spare a morsel of bread as alms for the poor. "There is no doubt whatever," he said, "that God took pity on me that night; for

somehow or other in these last two years I have been enabled
to escape from my drudgery. I was able to rent a tiny shop in
Sirus Avenue. Now I have been able to save enough to go on
this pilgrimage. My poor old father (God rest his soul and all
those who have passed away) was very anxious that I should
do this. "My dear boy," he said, "if ever the day comes when
you can go into that Great Presence, do not forget me, do not
forget me." He was my father. God has given him His mercy
and forgiveness. And indeed, now that I am going, I shall
remember his departed spirit, and I shall pray that from the
darkness of the tomb his spirit may befriend him."
    I was not the only one over whom my friend the grocer
poured his favors. The other passengers, too, shared the
warmth of his ceaseless flow of talk and of the stories he told
to amuse us. Now and again he would start singing. He had a
pleasant voice....

In "The Pilgrimage," his first published short story, Âl-e Ahmad
introduces themes that he will return to again and again in his writing:
Shi'i Islam and Persian Iranianness. As he is about to leave, he thinks
of the things people will do after he is gone, the special soup to be
served, the party to be held in his honor, and the prayers to be said there
for his safe return. His going to Iraq makes him all the more conscious
of the place he is leaving:

Well, that is Iran. And those are her customs: the vegetable
pilaw with fish on New Year's Eve, the New Year's display of
seven things that begin with the letter 's', the rice soup, the
samanu, the noodle soup, and a thousand other things like
them. Customs that at first sight seem silly, useless, trivial;
but which in reality are created by and conform to the pattern
of that special Iranian life . . . Oh Iran, Iran!

Persian culture is affirmed, the trip across the Iranian landscape
narrated, and other Iranians on the bus described. Then, all at once, the
reader is with Âl-e Ahmad inside the shrine at Karbalâ. There is no
mention of anything else: nothing of Iraq, nothing of Arabs, only the
Arabic language of the Quran. In a beautiful passage, Âl-e Ahmad
describes the language heard and seen inside the shrine:

Words from the Koran echoed and re-echoed beneath the lofty
domes. Those Arabic words poured out like rain and charged
the whole place with holiness. On doors and walls, on the
friezes, on the glasswork of the ceiling which reflected in
countless broken fragments the images of that vast crowd, on
the front and backs of Holy Books, on the prayer books in

men's hands, on the threshold of the sepulchre and all around
it, on the great silver padlocks of the Shrine—everywhere
those Arabic words were inscribed in thousands of designs and
figures and scrolls, on wood and tile, on brick, on silver, on
gold: everything was absorbed by their power. God knows
how many years these words have been there, looking down
upon all those who come and go, with importunity and with
indifference.

In effect, Âl-e Ahmad has managed to Iranicize Shi'i Islam as far
as he can. The narrator is obviously Persian, and all the other
characters are Iranian as well. The only country we see is Iran. Karbalâ
is experienced without Iraq. There are no Arabs and nothing Arab
except the Arabic language. "The Pilgrimage" is, in a sense, a
statement of Âl-e Ahmad's ideal of Iranian cultural identity. For while
he sees Shi'i Islam as essential to an Iranian cultural identity, Âl-e
Ahmad wants his Shi'ism de-Arabized in order to bring more sharply
into relief its "Iranian" character, although of course the origins of
Shi'ism and many of its followers are in fact Arab. In short, Âl-e
Ahmad strives to find in early Islam an Iranian connection, like Salmân
the Persian, and in contemporary Islam an Iranian connection with
Shi'ism, in order to represent Islam as an essentially non-Arab force.
(14)

Âl-e Ahmad's desire to Iranicize and de-Arabize, however, is
motivated as much by his disliking things Arab as by his liking things
Iranian. For Âl-e Ahmad is deeply prejudiced against Arabs, as is
clearly revealed in the short story "Al-Gomârak va al-Makus" [Customs
and Excise] (1949) (15), where Âl-e Ahmad shows the reader what he
had left hidden in "The Pilgrimage."

The narrator begins his story with his reaching the river where he
will cross to Basra, "where long boats with pointed bows were moored,
and headdressed Arabs, holding poles, were lined up babbling in
Arabic." He must share the boat with "a masked but nimble woman,
another policeman, two old men," and makes it across the river dizzy
but able to keep from getting sick. He describes the Arabs he sees:
"their strange nimbleness was unbelievable. I was deceived by their
long, constricting robes." The narrator recalls as well the taxi ride from
Khorramshahr to Ashar, where he had been cheated out of 18 tomâns.
Thus, Âl-e Ahmad introduces the themes which will run throughout the
story: Arabs as alien "others," their deceit, their greed, their crude
language, and his own disorientation, both physical and moral, brought
about in large part by the inhospitable, foreign, Arab, environment.

The narrator encounters Arab dishonesty and greed at every turn.
He had taken the train from Tehrân to Ahvâz, where the acquaintances

he made on the train had offered to take him across the river in a boat belonging to Shaykh 'Abbud. He refuses, not wanting to cross the border "illegally, with a bunch of smugglers." Instead, he takes a taxi from Khorramshahr to Ashar. He had paid 20 tomâns for the taxi, which he shared with five other passengers, two Australian soldiers and three Arabs. The driver tells him that the three Arabs own the taxi, and need not pay, and that he has to take the soldiers. The driver is Arab as well; his Persian is "strongly accented", and the narrator laughs to himself, until he discovers that the usual fare is only two tomâns, and he is embarrassed to have been cheated out of so much money. The boat man too is dishonest. He charges him half a dinar, but when he says he has not changed his money yet, he charges him four tomâns instead; however, half a dinar is worth seven and some tomâns. Apparently the boat man wants to get away with whatever he can, and the policeman standing nearby doesn't mind, for he gives no indication that the price is unfair.

In the customs house, his luggage is inspected by two officials, an old man and a younger man, who decide that he should pay duty on his soap and cloth, and pay as well for his books to be sent to Baghdad and examined for entry into Iraq. His camera is not allowed in at all, but the old man "who I thought didn't know Persian, took me aside and said quietly in my ear that he was prepared to buy it for 20 tomâns." As for the cotton cloth, his parents' burial shrouds, "it seemed they had found the customs duty for the cotton, or they had finally made it up themselves." The old man directs him to the moneychangers' bazaar, and offers again to buy his camera. The narrator "laughed in his face and walked off," not sure whether he "had laughed at his crude Persian, or was mocking his sharp-toothed greed."

The moneychanger the narrator visits

> was young, short and white, and looked more like a witless native of Mâzandarân than an Arab moneychanger from the Basra Bazaar. He spoke Persian quickly. I laughed to myself as he insisted that, if I had any more money, I should change it with him, and also that I find his associate in Baghdad, who would definitely give me a cheaper exchange rate.

Again it is unclear whether the narrator is laughing at the moneychanger's Persian or his greed.

When he returns to the customs house, he pays the tariffs, throwing the money onto the counter. But the young man still does not want to give him the receipt, and the old man whispers that the other wants half a dinar as a bribe. Outraged, the narrator "no longer laugh[s] at his crude Persian." Finally he swallows his "anger and hate" and the old man explains that then he will be allowed to take the camera. He pays and leaves.

It is not only the customs officials to whom the narrator objects; it is Arabic as well, when spoken by Arabs. The narrator knows some Arabic; when he sees the sign above the customs office, he tries to work out the meaning of a word he doesn't know from its root. Spoken Arabic, however, is "babbling." While the Arabs' poor Persian allows the narrator to feel superior, he finds it extremely frustrating to have to deal with Arabic; it is a strange and threatening linguistic environment. He hears the young customs official "muttering something in Arabic. I knew that he was swearing. I ignored it, but I was burning inside. It was torture." It seems to be the Arabic as much as the swearing and his own inability to respond which bothers him. He is able to convey his meaning in Persian, where he would not be able to in Arabic, when the narrator swears at the young man, "in his face with such anger and hate that he understood, and nearly jumped on the counter and punched me in the face." But how frustrating it is, when he feels the greatest need to express himself and communicate, by swearing, that he must do so in Persian, which the Arabs do not understand: "it was a pity they didn't understand." Later, however, he realizes the pointlessness of making himself understood, and while it is still frustrating, he is more resigned: "My curses were like grains of sand, curses which they didn't understand. It was just as well."

The narrator steps out of the customs house into an even more inhospitable physical environment:

> The asphalt of the street was scorching. I could still smell the sunburned leaves of the trees in the customs garden. I was terribly thirsty. I left the side of the pavement in the direction that I had been shown. My eyes, wide open, felt as if something was pressing from behind my eyeballs and that they were about to pop out. I didn't have a hat, and my collar was open. I didn't know what I had done with my handkerchief. I was dying of thirst.

His deliverance comes running in the form of the Persian boy Abdullah, a character set in sharp contrast against the greedy and dishonest Arabs of the story. When the boat man had overcharged the narrator, the boy had "gotten angry, and clenched his teeth so that the muscles in his cheeks stood out. It was as if he wanted to say something, but the border policeman stared at him...." And when Abdullah asks the narrator whether he would like to buy some cigarettes, his first thought is that the boy was getting ready to rob

him, seeing his "foreign appearance with neither headdress nor robes."
However, Abdullah's "anxious glance, and then his sweet Persian
ringing in my ear, put me right."

In fact, the narrator is overjoyed to have someone to talk to in
Persian:

> When I had been in the car from Khorramshahr to Basra, the
> three other passengers had talked continuously to the driver
> in Arabic. Only I and the two Australian soldiers had been
> silent. Nonetheless I hadn't felt like a stranger then. But as
> soon as I arrived at the hot and empty border police station, I
> had felt like an alien. Since then, whatever was spoken
> around me was strange and incomprehensible. Since then,
> wherever I went, all eyes were on me, and their fixed, curious
> gaze rested heavily on my face. All day, not only did I not
> understand whatever I heard, but it also made me angry. It was
> as if I had landed in a jail, and people were causing a
> commotion on the other side of its closed doors. Although I
> couldn't understand the meaning of the commotion, it
> certainly had to do with me, and was about me. But now a
> little door had opened in the middle of the thick wall of Arabic
> that had surrounded me and trapped me in its midst. A chink
> had been opened, a chink to my familiar environment, a little
> door through which a familiar sound was heard, leading me to
> happiness. A small door through which someone was
> speaking to me and about me in my own language.

Yet, while the narrator is happy to have someone to speak to in his
own language, the author unmistakably implies that since the boy is
Persian, he must be honest.

Abdullah tells the narrator that he had come there from
Mâzandarân and had been lost or left behind by his mother some years
ago. The Arabs do not call him Abdullah, however, but *welek*, "hey
you." The author goes on to imply Arab vice as well: "He told me that
on the very first day the police had taken him here and there, but that
they had bothered him so much at nights that he had run away from
them."

Abdullah goes out of his way to help the narrator in this strange
and foreign city, taking him to the money changers' market. The
narrator offers to take Abdullah back to Iran with him, if he should
return this way, and tells him to wait for him while he finishes his
business at the customs office. But when he comes out, it is late, so
he runs to the taxi stand to get to the train station to buy his ticket. He
is still swearing at all customs officials, and again describes the
oppressive environment:

> The tops of the high walls lining the backstreets were close together, pressing the hot afternoon air of Basra down where I was quickly passing. It was a pressing heat, and once again I felt that my eyesockets were wide open, as if something was pressing on my eyeballs from behind. I imagined that my eyeballs were about to jump out and splatter in front of me on the hot ground of the backstreets of Basra.

The narrator has forgotten all about Abdullah. He jumps into the taxi, which is full, but "Arabs rolled up their robes, moved and made room for me somehow." Then Abdullah arrives, out of breath. The taxi pulls away, and the boy stands there, forcing himself to smile. The narrator hesitates, and then does nothing, does not smile at him or even say goodbye; he feels upset and impotent. He knows he should have done something, but apparently the strange and hostile environment, with its dishonest and greedy customs officials, Arabs speaking Arabic, and its heat has so affected him that he is unable to do the right thing:

> Oh, how these Arabic terms, these Arabic names with their difficult letters to pronounce brought out the worst in me. How much *'ayn* and *qâf* from the back of the throat. How many *tayn*s and *zayn*s from the middle of the tongue! But how quickly we reached the station! It was a long way. I didn't notice how far we had come, but the sharp, bad-smelling cigarette of a headdressed Arab sitting next to me was finished.

He buys some tea in the station tea room, and sits drinking it completely alienated from the people around him, who are not "people," but "Arabs":

> Arabs were sitting crosslegged on the benches, leaving their sandals in front of them on the ground. The air was buzzing, thick with the sharp smell of Arabs' cigarettes, and waterpipes, each with eight or ten mouthpieces, surrounded by Arabs.
>
> The coffee seller had laid out his things in a corner of this rough hall on two big tables. His assistant was moving among the Arabs with a brass coffee pot, pouring their bitter black coffee, drop by drop, into their cups.

The narrator tries to distract himself from thinking about Abdullah and his own unkindness toward him, and tries to paint a different, more positive picture of the situation he finds himself in, where people and things around him are all right. The reality of the situation, however, cannot be denied: the reality, according to the author, of the Arabs as hateful and hated others, and of the complete and utter alienation of the Persian narrator from them and their world. Even allowing for culture shock, Âl-e Ahmad makes it clear that there can be no common human ties between them:

> However much I tried to calm myself and watch the people happily and easily pouring the black, bitter drops of coffee onto their tongues, holding its taste for a while in their mouths, I just couldn't. Everything was tiresome. Everything made me uncomfortable. Whatever I looked at pressed heavily on my eyes. I wanted to order a coffee, but I was afraid. I still didn't know whether I could drink this thick black Arab coffee or not. My short meeting with the boy cigarette seller at the Basra customs, the consolation which this short meeting had given me, my behavior towards him, and my abandoning him in the end without any kindness, attention, or saying goodbye, badly troubled me. I wanted to cry. I wanted to find someone to talk to, to complain to. But the faces of the headdressed Arabs pouring the bitter black coffee onto their tongues and sucking it, were so repulsive, and so rough that they revolted me, I was disgusted.

While Âl-e Ahmad's "animus toward the Arabs" (16) reminds one of Hedâyat, Âl-e Ahmad's Iranianness differs from that of Hedâyat. He does not readily accept the ideology of Aryanism, or the view of history to which it gave rise. In *Plagued by the West*, Âl-e Ahmad refers to "Aryan studies quackery" and refers to Iranians as "we who escaped from India (if this is in fact true)." (17) Âl-e Ahmad dismisses the Pahlavi regime's nationalism as "new forms of drugs to lull the people into political quiescence." (18) One of these is "The Delusion of Grandeur Syndrome":

> This occurs because an insignificant individual sees his own greatness in the grandeur which is falsely ascribed to him in national pageants, extravagant festivals, tinsel victory arches, crown jewels kept in the vault of the National Bank.... In short, in anything that will please the eye and that will puff up an insignificant man so that he will imagine himself to be great.

Another is "The Delusion about Ancient Grandeur Syndrome: Pretentious bragging—foolish self-glorification—Cyrus the Great and Darius!—self aggrandizement based on irrelevant past glories." (19)

Yet while he rejects "Aryanism," Âl-e Ahmad puts forward an Islamic Iranian history where again he attempts to Iranicize and de-Arabize Islam as far as is possible. Arabs are scorned, and true Islam emerged only when it reached the Persian empire: "As for Islam, it was only when it reached the area between the Tigris and Euphrates [then the political and cultural centre of the Sâsânid empire] that it became true Islam. Before that it was merely the nomadism and jaheliyyat [period of ignorance] of the Arabs." (20)

Âl-e Ahmad further dissociates Islam from its Arab roots:

> And if we examine the facts a little more impartially, we shall see that Islam itself was yet another movement based on the demands of urban people living between the Euphrates and Syria who had grown tired of the long wars betwen Iran and the Byzantine Empire. With the longing of parched animals, they thirsted after calm and would have become the supporters of any movement which could make a prolonged peace in that region grow. We know that, in his youth, the Prophet traded with Syria and that he spoke with a certain monk there. And was there ever any easier way to proselytize than with the cry "Say: There is no God but Allah and ye shall prosper." (21)

Âl-e Ahmad's view of history is similar to Saffârzâdeh's; in contrast to the more popular view, Islam did not so much conquer Iran, but rather,

> we ourselves invited it to Iran. Let us admit that it was really Rostam [son of] Farrokhzâd [the commander of the Persian army at the battle of Qadesiyya] who struggled in vain to defend the Sâsânid cavalry and the petrified rites of Zoroastrianism; whereas the people of Ctesiphon stood in the streets, holding dates and bread to welcome the Arab advance troops who had come to plunder the royal palace and the Bahârestân carpet. (22)

In fact, Âl-e Ahmad refuses to glorify the Persian empire, not only as a monarchy but also as a period of historic glory, suggesting that perhaps we will understand why Iranians turned to Islam "once we have learned what incredible injustices were visited on people as a result of the ossified customs of the Sâsânids." (23)

Islam is presented as being essentially Iranian from its beginnings, depending upon an Iranian, Salmân the Persian, for its initial development, and reaching back even earlier to share the ideals of Mazdak and Mâni:

Salmân-e Fârsi, years before Yazdegerd fled Marv, escaped from Jay in Isfahan and found refuge in Medina with the Muslims and played such an important role in the development of Islam that, in comparison, it completely overshadows the role of the Magi astronomers in the development of Christianity. I do not feel, therefore, that we can view Islam as a world conqueror in the way that we see Alexander as world conqueror. The mercenary, unbridled soldiers of that Macedonian leader were all exiles from their own native lands and had come here in search of plunder. Not one of them concealed the kind of faith in their quivers that drew the barefoot Arabs all the way to the Oxus and Jaxartes. Notwithstanding the ideas of our bearded and mustachioed learned, who are a kind of latter-day Sho'ubiyya, and in spite of Omar's book burners in Ray and Alexandria, Islam was a resounding, if belated "yes" to a summons which began centuries earlier in the wastelands of former kingdoms—a summons which, in the forms of Manichaeism and Mazdakism was nipped in the bud and stifled in the mouth of their founders with hot lead. (24)

The later development of Islam, too, is described as being essentially Iranian. While some facts of Arab domination cannot be ignored, and are in fact resented, it is in contrast to and indeed against this Arab presence that Iranicized Islam developed. Indeed, Âl-e Ahmad suggests that without the Iranian contribution, Islam would not have become a great, and overwhelmingly Iranian, civilization:

But is it not just as true that today we are just another puppet state of the West? And is it not also true that from the beginning of the Islamic movement until six or seven centuries afterwards we played the same role? While ostensibly we were one of the provinces of the Baghdad Caliphate (in the guise of being a part of an Islamic totality), what share in the Islamic world did we have? And again, is it not a fact that even in the darkest years of Omayyad domination, we, relying on our identity as a people and the Iranian style which we lent to Islam, carried the black banner of the Abbasids from Khorâsân to Baghdad. We so Iranicized Islamic civilization that even today inexperienced orientalists are stymied when trying to determine what percentage of the components of Islamic civilization are non-Iranian. (25)

Yet here again, in the conclusion of *Plagued by the West* as in "The Pilgrimage," Âl-e Ahmad affirms the Arabic language: "Therefore I will end by purifying my pen with this verse from the Quran: 'The hour of resurrection drew near and the moon was rent in twain'...." (26)

While Âl-e Ahmad rejects Arabs, he does not reject the Arabic language of the Quran; it is seen as something separate from the Arabs, as belonging not to them but rather to God as the language of revelation. We will see the same feelings toward the Arabic language in *Lost in the Crowd*.

Khasi dar Miqât [Lost in the Crowd] (1966) is an account of the pilgrimage Âl-e Ahmad made to Mecca in 1964, based on the journal he kept while on his trip, and in it Âl-e Ahmad reveals himself as a most unusual pilgrim. He has not prayed for some twenty years previous. He repeatedly asks why he is going on this trip, and mentions that most of his friends would make fun of his going: "Iranian intellectuals spurn these events, and walk among them gingerly and with distaste. 'The Hajj?' they say. 'Don't you have anywhere else to go?'" (27) Throughout the book, there is hardly any thought or mention of God, or of any religious concepts such as the human soul, good, evil, or forgiveness. The very act of keeping a journal helps to maintain his stance as a largely ironic observer, rather than a devout participant. (28)

Âl-e Ahmad's faith is qualified, even in the statement of his wife, Simin Dâneshvar:

> If he turned to religion, it was the result of his wisdom and insight because he had previously experimented with Marxism, socialism, and, to some extent, existentialism and his relative return to religion and the Hidden Imam was a way toward deliverance from the evil of imperialism and toward the preservation of national identity, a way toward human dignity, compassion, justice, reason, and virtue. Jalâl had need of such a religion. (29)

In *Lost in the Crowd*, Âl-e Ahmad says he made the pilgrimage "mostly out of curiosity" (30); he describes his coming as "neither a trick nor a matter of a lamb and the flock. It was something entirely different. The lost sheep had now turned into a mangy goat that simply wished to hide himself in the crowd." (31) He compares his understanding of the nature of the pilgrimage, his being "just a 'piece of straw' that had come to the 'Miqât'," to the understanding of "that other atheist, Mayhaneh'i, or Bastâmi," who told the hajji, "Put your sack of money down, circumambulate me, and go back home." (32) And one may consider as well Âl-e Ahmad's own statement in *Plagued by the West*, that "all of them [Iranians] are waiting for the twelfth Imam to appear. That is, WE are all waiting for him and rightly so. Except each of us in our own way." (33)

While Âl-e Ahmad may have seen Shi'i Islam as essential to his definition of Iranianness, and so as that which could resolve his cultural conflicts and dilemmas, (34), he presents his personal religious belief as problematic. His keeping a journal of the trip in itself reveals that he considered himself to be going more as an observer than a participant. In fact, those few occasions when he does begin to feel "lost in the crowd" are extremely unpleasant for him, and he removes himself from those situations:

> This sa'y between Safaa and Marveh stupefies a man. It takes you right back to 1400 years ago, to 10.000 years ago, ...this great engulfing of the individual in the crowd.... Before today, I thought it was only the sun that could not be regarded with the naked eye, but I realized today that neither can one look at this sea of eyes ... and fled, after only two laps. You can easily see what an infinity you create in that multitude from such nothingness, and this is when you are optimistic, and have just begun. If not, in the presence of such infinity you see you are less than nothing. Like a particle of rubbish on the ocean, no, on an ocean of people, or perhaps a bit of dust in the air. To put it more clearly, I realized I was going crazy. I had an urge to break my head open against the first concrete pillar. (35)

The same concern, this conflict between the mass and the individual, was expressed in "Seh'târ," where religion is set against individual existence, and Islam is portrayed as that which interferes with one's behavior. Given such an understanding of religious experience, the journal is a self-defense mechanism as well, allowing Âl-e Ahmad to remain uninvolved except on his own terms. Perhaps, very sadly, he is afraid to surrender to the event and find in the end that he does not truly believe, afraid to make that leap of faith and fail; better in that case to leave the question unanswered.

Yet Âl-e Ahmad does believe in Islam as a tool against the West, having the potential to provide great unity among the oppressed against Western exploitation; and more specifically he believes in Shi'i Islam as an essential component of an Iranian national identity. Yet Âl-e Ahmad wishes to be both pan-Islamist and Iranian nationalist, a difficult position to hold, and the only way he can hold it and resolve the contradiction is, again, as in *Plagued by the West*, to de-Arabize Islam, and instead create a larger, Asian identity into which Islam will fit. Accordingly, he theorizes, "Is the ihram itself basically anything other than a sari? The pause at Mash'ar al-Haram has its origins in Buddhism." (36) Of course it is more than fortuitous chance that this larger Asian identity is basically Indian; he knows very well the "Aryan" connection he is making, as he does as well when he discusses the Islamic prophets and their relation to the Semitic tribes, contrasting this with "our own mythology" of Keyumars and so on. (37) Yet, in reading *Lost in the Crowd*, one must conclude that Âl-e Ahmad has another reason as well for wanting to de-Arabize Islam: his own prejudice against Arabs.

Âl-e Ahmad is very conscious of the different nationalities of the people he meets, and in fact is eager to differentiate among them. But it seems clear that Âl-e Ahmad's concept of "nationality" includes some notion of "race." One may note that his definition of Iranianness includes language, culture and religion; on the other hand, in *Plagued by the West*, he refers to "my Afghan neighbors and I, who share the same religion, race, and language." (38) Just as the anti-Arab feelings Âl-e Ahmad expresses are typical of many 20th century secular (Persian) Iranian intellectuals, (39) one may assume that he shared as well, to some extent at least, other wide-spread, pseudo-scientific ideas such as there being "Aryan" or "Semitic" races. On the other hand, Âl-e Ahmad, like Jamâlzâdeh, is a *sayyed*, a descendant of the Prophet Mohammed, and so theoretically has some "Arab blood." Perhaps this fact keeps him from subscribing too wholeheartedly to racial theories. Yet the distinctions he makes among nationalities correspond to those that would be made along "racial" rather than ethnic, cultural or linguistic lines. Thus, in a food concessions market he observes "blacks, Arabs, Turks and Iranians" (40); visiting the maritime Hajj Village, he relates:

> There is an Indian ship docked there with hajjis unloading, the simplest of hajjis, and the least encumbered. They come wrapped in saris, wearing loin cloths, and carrying tea kettles for drinking, steeping tea, and washing. Iranians carry aftabehs; Turks have long tubes with bulbous ends that look like tin kerosene lamps. The Lebanese and Syrians have plastic aftabehs that are smaller than ours—and the Indians and Africans carry kettles. These are the most meaningful national emblems, and they aren't found on flags, but in peoples' hands. And how handy they are! (41)

Still, it is not easy to tell some of these nationalities apart. Some of Âl-e Ahmad's fellow travellers are "Turks from Arâk" who speak Persian poorly (42), and when someone addresses Âl-e Ahmad in Turkish, he remarks, "People take me for a Turk all the time. The barber next to the alfalfa market thought I was a Turk too." (43)

Most revealing of his racial thinking are Âl-e Ahmad's observations on the Blacks he sees; they are also the most difficult to fit into his racial scheme. He finds them exotic and fascinating: "they have the most interesting faces of the Hajj. Especially when they are wearing the white ihram. The whiteness of the ihram and the blackness of their skin are poetically beautiful." (44) On the other hand, his own standards of beauty are such that the face of a "stunningly beautiful" Black woman from Cameroon "didn't have Negro characteristics" (45); the implication is that if she did look "Negro," she wouldn't be beautiful.

Âl-e Ahmad finds Blacks "picturesque" in praying: "They sprawled out so much for *tashahhod* that one would have thought incapable of sitting on their knees." (46) He finds in this a racial/national significance, as he "realized at that prayer that the custom of kneeling is an ancient one that comes from Asia, from Islam, India, Buddhism, Japan, China, and other parts of that area. Neither the Europeans nor the Africans have mastered it." (47)

The problem, of course, is how to classify Black Arabs, for here racial categories overlap and break down, and in fact Âl-e Ahmad tends to treat them as a category by themselves. He mentions seeing "a local black-skinned Arab" in a coffee house, (48) and a "tall black Arab" preaching in Medina (49). He also talks about the Nakhawalahs, a Shi'i sect in Medina which claims descent from Bilal, the Ethiopian companion and muezzin of the Prophet Muhammad. (50) In fact, his deceased brother's local guide had been a Nakhawalah, Ahmad ibn Wa'il, and Âl-e Ahmad has lunch with him at his home in Medina; he mentions that his host "had gone to a great deal of trouble and expense," to provide for his guests. (51)

But most of the time Âl-e Ahmad is sure of himself when it comes to Arabs. He mentions praying in the street near a woman who "wore a white mantle and didn't look Arab" (52); later, he mentions an old man, "evidently not an Arab." (53) One can only wonder what criteria he employs in determining who "looks" Arab. In fact, as in "Customs and Excise," he tends to refer to the Arabs he sees as Arabs, rather than men or women, shopkeepers or students; clearly the fact of their being Arab, and other, is uppermost in his mind. In one innocently revealing passage, Âl-e Ahmad describes date groves on the outskirts of Medina, with, not farmers, but "Arabs going to and fro with radios that played songs in [surprisingly enough] Arabic." (brackets added) (54)

Âl-e Ahmad goes so far as to distinguish between different Arab nationalities—Syrian, Saudi, and so on—perhaps because pan-Arabism does not fit his definition of nationality. For while Âl-e Ahmad defines nationality in terms of language, culture and traditions (55), he defines it in terms of race as well, and he sees racial differences between Syrians and Lebanese, who he claims have fairer complexions (56), Saudis, and Black Arabs. He describes the Yemeni Arabs he encounters in particular detail: "Each of the Yemenis, filthy, with tangled hair, sunken eyes, and a rope tied around the waist, looks like another John the Baptist, risen from the grave." (57) In addition, they are "very rough." (58) Later he has a conversation with three Yemenis, who "couldn't comprehend maps and weren't even literate.... It appears that these Yemenis are the poorest of all the pilgrims in the world. They're all ragged and excessively thin from poor nutrition. These people are the ones who've been having a real feast the last two or three days in the vicinity of the slaughterhouse." (59) Later, he goes to the market, looking for the fabric merchants, and buys cloth from another Yemeni, "a young man with a beard, good-looking and charming, [who] was quite courteous." (60) They drink tea together and discuss politics, even though "his Engrish was worse than my Arabic." (61)

Âl-e Ahmad is equally conscious of the different sects he encounters, and throughout the book asks people what school they belong to. Usually Âl-e Ahmad concludes that they do not know, or that they are mistaken. In a conversation with three Saudi high school students, "when I asked if they were Hanafi, Maliki, or what else, they were stumped at first. Then they thought about it and one of them said Hanbali. He was obviously talking nonsense. The contagion of irreligion is everywhere." (62) The Hanbali school of law, however, is the official school of Saudi Arabia. (63)

Yet even while Âl-e Ahmad is sensitive to Sunni/Shi'i differences, it is often difficult to say whether it is so much that as it is Arab/Persian differences. He relates other people's anecdotes, about a man praying in the Prophet's Mosque who wouldn't change his place because he would have to begin his prayers again, and about another man who broke wind right before praying, but went ahead and began his prayers anyway, without the required ablutions, and calls such stories "the usual Shi'i humor and mockery at the expense of the Sunnis." (64) Later, though, his brother-in-law Javâd tells of seeing

> an Arab squatting beside one of the stoning pillars ... relieving himself in the middle of the milling crowd. An Esfahâni in our group said "This hajji gentleman must have been rockless, and had to dump some manure to throw at Satan." Another said the man must really hate Satan ... and this sort of clowning around. (65)

In fact anti-Arab prejudice is so commonplace that Âl-e Ahmad doesn't give it a second thought. On the way to Medina, the group's bus breaks down repeatedly, and when other drivers in the group offer to help, the driver refuses. Âl-e Ahmad's comment is, "Arab blockheadedness." (66)

> The people became loud and agitated, the women whining and swearing, especially cursing everything Arab. It reached a point where I intervened once or twice, yelling at this one or that one "why have you lost control of yourself this way?" Other passing vehicles stopped occasionally to sympathize or help, but the driver was stubborn, or else unauthorized or in danger of being docked part of his pay. (67)

Even though Âl-e Ahmad speculates that the driver might have other reasons for refusing help, he does not retract his own explanation of "Arab stubbornness."

Âl-e Ahmad, however, does not refer to women as Arabs. Apparently men are Arabs, while women are women; men are the bearers of nationality, while women's province is sex. So he describes how "an Arab man was bending over kissing the hand of a woman dressed in black, through the window of an automobile.... I think they were Syrians. Behaving like the French bourgeoisie right on the Plain of 'Arafat!" (68)

Still, Âl-e Ahmad's portrayal of Arab women is largely unflattering. He describes how "the local women" carry their children on their hips, so "the child looks like he's riding a camel, one foot on the mother's stomach, the other on her back." (69) But Âl-e Ahmad sees Arab women more in terms of their sexuality than anything else. The first definitely Arab woman he describes is a beggar on the way to Uhud, early in the morning:

> There was a beautiful young woman begging, wearing a cloth mask over her nose and mouth. As she approached I saw a glint in her eye that ought not to be seen during the Hajj season. And such eyes! Just like the eyes of a deer, of which you have read in so much poetry. But as they say, you had to be there. Her black gown was very thin, and beneath it she wore a long tattered shirt. She must have been cold. Her small, erect breasts did not move beneath her shirt. I was cold myself. I was wearing nothing but a long shirt, thinking I was in Saudi Arabia where it is warm. Too early in the morning face to face with a woman like that. (70)

He describes a school bus, "full of ripe young girls in smocks," (71) and some older school girls:

> They had cape-like mantles over their shoulders, tucked around the neck and open in front, with their colored or white blouses visible beneath them. Sometimes when they opened or fastened the opening in front of the cape or shook hands, the young buds on their chests were visible. They wore scarves on their heads, made of black muslin, just like big hats. Their socks and shoes were both white. The truth is that the first thing that caught my eye was the color of their shoes, and then my gaze moved higher. (72)

And later, in Mecca, Âl-e Ahmad describes another girl:

> The real Mecca must be seen in this quarter, and in these streets. The road itself is a sewer, and there is filth and trash in every corner. In the midst of this setting sat a 14- to 15-year-old girl on the balcony of her house opening and closing her gown, showing her white thighs and calves. The opportunity to see women is truly rare here. (73)

Following his conversation with three male high school students, freshmen or sophomores, Âl-e Ahmad goes so far as to assert that,

> you can't blame the Saudis for having more homosexuality than any other place in the world. There probably haven't been more than one or two unveiled women since I left Tehran, and even fewer who were pretty. Those three young men were quite handsome, with beautiful smiles. One of them spoke with a womanly suggestiveness. Only one had a deep male voice. (74)

The reader might note that it would not be unusual for fourteen- or fifteen-year-old boys to have high voices. And, of course, one can only wonder what sources Âl-e Ahmad had reference to in determining the incidence of homosexuality in Saudi Arabia as compared to the rest of the world. His assertion that there are few, if any, "pretty" Arab women (because he hasn't seen any), like Hedâyat, follows from his sexist view of women, and racist view of Arabs.

Perhaps the overriding impression Âl-e Ahmad has of Arabs is that they are "primitive." While Âl-e Ahmad's reference to the pilgrims leaving Tehrân as "these people who have answered the primal call of a desert religion" (75) might be taken ironically in the context it appears, comparing the more laughable, old-fashioned, but more authentic Iranians going on Hajj with those going to Europe, he undercuts whatever irony it held only a few lines later, when their airplane is flying over the desert and he remarks, "No trace of civilization. Sand, sand, sand. I wearied of it." (76)

Âl-e Ahmad sees primitivism and backwardness everywhere in Saudi Arabia. Even the architecture of the mosque of Abu Bakr, Omar, Ali and Zahra in Medina "has been preserved by primitive will power." (77) In order to fit in, Âl-e Ahmad buys a canvas water bottle "that resembles the style of the leather ones. It makes one feel more primitive." (78) Yet even that is unnecessary:

> An Arab came and went as I was lying down on a blanket under the lifeless shadow of the canopy. He tied a rope around the neck of a primus stove and went off swinging it, like a water bottle or a piece of crockery. Even Western industrial products can be adapted to primitive consumption. (79)

And when he first arrives, he has to change his clothes to something more appropriate: "Obviously, the soles of the feet and the top of the head must be carefully protected from [not the sun, but] the primitive life." (brackets added) (80) So he buys a *dishdasha* and *kaffiyah*, but even the clothes are unsatisfactory. He finds the *dishdasha* "delightful, like a cone of sugar cubes," (81) a rather frivolous image for men's clothing, but in fact it is a frivolous piece of clothing, for it is too tight in the shoulders, both for Âl-e Ahmad and his companion, the "Turk from Arâk." (82) Furthermore, Âl-e Ahmad has to split open the sides to be able to sit and stand. (83) Later, his feet swell up from sitting so long on the bus, but he suspects "it's the result of running around with exposed legs." (84) The implication is that he would prefer not to dress like an Arab, if he had any choice: when he goes for a walk wearing "an Arab head cloth over my head like a scarf.... There is no alternative. It was so dusty! And so sunny!" (85)

Âl-e Ahmad finds Arabs and their environment not only primitive, but also dirty. From the time of his arrival, Âl-e Ahmad complains about the filthy toilets provided for the pilgrims: "The toilet here is also disgraceful. It's a cement pit, with five positions separated by partitions and a half-open wooden door. There's a line at the door from morning until night. And such a stench in the air! Five privies for five 100-person groups!" (86)

In Medina, he visits the Garden of Purity, where the public toilet is dirtier than the dirtiest toilet in Iran: "The Shâh Mosque was 100 times cleaner 20 years ago." (87) The garden itself is unsatisfactory: "it was nothing but a decrepit old date orchard, with water from a pump house above it pouring into a pool.... And such dirt, heat, and filth! Just like *sizdahbedar* at an Emâmzâdeh Davud in a Sousa date orchard." (88)

He also remarks of Medina, "And these flies! I've never seen the like in my life, not even is Khorramshahr, not even in Sagzabad before the advent of DDT—to mention only a few places. (89) Mecca, however, is even filthier:

> But there was such filth in the high streets that led to the Abu Qabis Mosque. The real Mecca must be seen in this quarter, and in these streets. The road itself is a sewer, and there is filth and trash in every corner. (90)
> Beside Mt. Safa—outside the House of God—they've built a large underground toilet. Recently. I went to look at it. Such stench, and such a crowd, and not one bit of ventilation, not even one window. They could easily put in a fan, but who thinks about these things? Of importance is the fact that I don't know where the Mecca sewage disposal plant is located. In this city of stone, one cannot dig a well. I don't think they have sewage pipes, either. What do they do, then? Isn't this the basic reason for the city's filth? (91)

Here, while suggesting that the environment is such that it is difficult to dispose of filth, Âl-e Ahmad assumes as well that no one thinks of doing anything about it.

> This Muslim *qebleh* is a pitiful thing. No one cares about the sanitary conditions in the area around it. If we were to adhere to Meccan standards of cleanliness—especially during the Hajj season (what do I know about how it is the rest of the year?)—for the Muslim world, it would be most unworthy of the Muslims. One must see Mecca and the Bedouin Arab-turned-urbanite's life without water in order to understand what it means to have ablutions five times a day. All these religious precepts concerning cleanness and uncleanness are to control the filth you see in those streets. But how long will this go on for, anyway? After 1,400 years, and with all these modernizing facilities for pipelines, sewage, and sanitation, if you look at old Mecca it's still like the Jewish quarter of Esfahân. It's worse than ancient Dezful, with those toilets on the rooftops. When you climb up the steps on those Meccan streets you can see how and why the rabble threw trash at the Prophet. (92)

Yet, in spite of the filth, Âl-e Ahmad notes that,

The Arabs here have much healthier eyes than those I saw in Iraq in 1943. Is this due to the difference in locale? Or the result of medical care, and the better hygiene that has been practiced in the last 20 years in this part of the world. Whatever it is, eye ailments have been eliminated. The old people are still blind or with poor eyesight, most of them. Adolescents and younger, however, have large, black, shining eyes. (93)

Nevertheless, he makes it clear that the people hardly know how to manage their environment. When Âl-e Ahmad describes the trees planted along the road to Uhud, he remarks, "What a blessing each is in a desert like Saudi Arabia. Even the Saudis know the value of trees." (94) Still, as Âl-e Ahmad makes clear, it is Arabs to which he objects, not so much the environment. Âl-e Ahmad's party leaves Arafat for Mina long after everyone else has gone:

We ate dinner on a carpet of sand, outside the tents, beneath the sky, when our belongings were in the truck, the other people had gone, and the feeling of this one day of Bedouin life in the open spaces was coming alive. The tents—now that the people aren't here to separate you from the environment with their trampling—are quite beautiful. I walked among them. They are like capsized ships, the guy lines their oars, and they are in sand instead of water. (Thus it was not for nothing that Manochehri became the "Poet of the Desert.") The remains of this Bedouin picnic consisted of campfire ashes, the remains of carcasses, and little piles of bones. There is no sign of a dog or a cat. What would happen if we stayed here 1 or 2 more days? (95)

Most interesting is the suggestion of the dangerously seductive beauty of the primitive life. Perhaps if they stayed they would never make it back to civilization.

In keeping with their primitivism, Âl-e Ahmad sees Arabs as violent and ill-mannered as well:

An old blind Arab passed, with a cane as thin as a finger, undoubtedly made of bamboo. Another old Arab who wanted a ride accosted a driver. The driver hit him in the chest so hard that the food in my mouth turned to rock. They're so very violent. I saw something even worse in the Prophet's sanctuary: A young man and his wife were walking along holding onto each other. The crowd separated the woman from her husband for a moment. The man went back and hit a

> white-skinned (Syrian or Lebanese) woman who was between
> him and his wife in the back hard with the palm of his hand.
> He snatched his wife's wrist so violently with the other hand
> that I was sure her hand had come loose. They are dangerously
> violent. They talk much too loudly. And how their drivers
> blare their horns! (96)

According to Âl-e Ahmad, this violence occurs officially as well,
in the form of police brutality. At the Baqi' Cemetery, "the police were
chasing the hajjis out, and with brutality and force. The end of visiting
hours? No doubt." (97) At Uhud,

> Berber and Bedouin women came and pushed themselves
> closer through the crowd. When they saw that the police were
> a little ways away they would snatch a fistful of dirt from the
> grave and run, the police swearing in hot pursuit, brandishing
> their headbands like whips in their hands. Javâd was upset
> very much by this. At one point he finally took one of them
> by the collar and said in Arabic "You're a dog! You're a Jew!"
> I didn't think he had it in him. (98)

Later, "there was little protest from the police against all of Javâd's
remonstrations. As it turns out, the Saudis are not as praetorian this
year." (99)   Yet later Âl-e Ahmad qualifies his charges of police
brutality:

> A man was rattling the silver grill work around Sultan Salim's
> grave so hard (the Imam's tomb is raised above floor level)
> that I thought he was going to shake it loose. He was asking
> for something. Sometimes, therefore, the police are justified
> in what they do. (100)

In *Plagued by the West*, Âl-e Ahmad had referred to "Ibn Sa'ud
with all the excesses of his pre-Islamic-age kingdom (the chopping off
of hands and heads)." (101) Now, throughout *Lost in the Crowd*, he
accuses the Saudi government of stupidity, primitivism, inefficiency,
and greed. Here, the Arab Other works as a metaphor for Iran: criticism
of the Saudi regime serves as an indirect criticism of the Pahlavi
regime as a monarchy as well, necessarily indirect because of Iranian
censorship. (102) However, his criticism of the Saudi government has
an anti-Arab component as well. Throughout the book, Âl-e Ahmad
complains about the poor quality or outright lack of facilities for the
Hajj, from busses to lodging to toilets:

During the time we sat in the bus waiting to leave Jedda, we saw what a lot of porters there are, and how many poor people in the villages along the road, and most of them blind and paralyzed! But God save us from Jedda and its porters! It appears that the brunt of the weight of the Hajj rites is carried on the shoulders of the porters. Porters who have no straps or harnesses, only their empty hands. So pointless! They used their teeth to untie the brand-new spools the driver had given them for tying up loads; they placed the section to be cut on the asphalt and spent a full ten minutes severing it with a piece of rock. They didn't even have a pocket knife.... It is true that the task of transporting 800,000 foreigners in less than a month is not a simple one for a country whose population is only 5 or 6 times that number. Nonetheless, it's obvious that no facilities are prepared beforehand for the Hajj. They have left the matter of the Hajj to the most backward, primitive, untutored, and poverty-stricken layers of society. (103)

Âl-e Ahmad complains as well about the poverty he sees around him, describing the "legions of beggars" (104) he sees everywhere in Saudi Arabia:

And God save us from the beggars. Women, children, old and young. Not only the blind, paralyzed, and the crippled, but healthy ones too. In a one-hour walk, all the pocket change I had disappeared. (105)

Then there are these itinerant merchants, who circulate among the tents in little groups. And all kinds of beggars, beggars, beggars. I don't have the energy to describe them one by one. Only one of them was interesting, an Arab woman with a long written Arabic explanation of her problems that said she was eligible to receive both khoms and zakat and with the signature and seal of some Arab religious magistrate. Some had shoes, some did not, and the ones without them were filthier than those with. There are ice vendors, cigarette merchants, orange sellers, beggars, sellers of games, beggars, beggars, and beggars. All claiming to working for God. (106)

He is insightful enough to conclude that it is not merely "Arab backwardness" which is responsible for such poverty, but that there are more compelling social, political and economic reasons: "The poor people that thrive parasitically on the Hajj and its pilgrims, and serve as its porters are so beneficial to the antiquated Saudi system, and such a well-established institution, that I don't think they'll take steps to eliminate their poverty so soon" (107);

> I wondered what was the source of this legendary Saudi Arabian security, and whether the stories one hears are true. Hajjis have no need to steal. They are usually rich, and have come to visit shrines or worship. But what about the local people? There is an abundance of beggars and poor people, and porters, porters, porters. No one, however, has said anything as yet about theft. There are no soldiers in sight. Police, however, patrol everywhere, even inside the Prophet's Mosque, and their presence is somewhat irritating. (108)

Âl-e Ahmad never sees anyone who has had a hand or foot amputated, but he is apparently compelled to mention it (as he had in *Plagued by the West*), referring to it not as a punishment prescribed by Islamic law but as a backward Saudi Arabian custom:

> A crippled man with a crutch under this arm came and sat on the cool sand in the House.... At first I thought he was one of those who had his foot amputated for theft according to Saudi custom (it seems they still administer punishments of this type) but when he sat down I saw it was inherited. He had a deformed and shriveled foot. (109)

Indeed, in most of his criticism of the Saudi government, the anti-Arab animus seems to have the upper hand. Remarking on the shortage of doctors and hospital beds in Saudi Arabia, in spite of the revenues generated by oil and the Hajj, Âl-e Ahmad concludes, "Here's to the health of these ignorant Arabs that rule this corner of the world in the name of Islam." (110); later, he describes a Bleeding Doctor at work, another token of the primitive state of Saudi health care. (111) And he asserts that those oil revenues "are your only means of rising above life in tents to a government of prejudice." (112)

But again, it is not just the government of Saudi Arabia to which he objects; Âl-e Ahmad finds it hard to accept any expression of Saudi Arab nationalism, and implies that such expressions are empty and immature. He reports that "the local Arabic newspapers were full of boastful pride today because the Kaaba's shroud was made by the Saudis themselves this year, and they did not accept one from the Egyptians." (113) He describes the high school students he talks to as "young people, infatuated with Arab nationalism and the power it will have." (114) And in questioning the information offered him by his taxi driver in Jedda concerning the population of Jedda and of Saudi

Arabia, Âl-e Ahmad remarks in a footnote, "In any case, as a patriot (though an Arab), he had the right to show off, put on airs, and so on for a foreign tourist." (115)   Here, however, Âl-e Ahmad's attitude toward Arab nationalism seems to be much the same as his attitude, in *Plagued by the West*, toward official Pahlavi Iranian nationalism; he sees it as a delusion, used to distract the people and keep the rulers in power.

Âl-e Ahmad reveals more of his political thinking in a long conversation later on, with a young Saudi army officer. Âl-e Ahmad begins by describing the man in what can only be described as racist fashion: "He was an Anizah Arab. I never thought an Anizah could be just like a human being, and so neat." (116) It turns out that the man is a communist, and their conversation turns to politics. Âl-e Ahmad pauses to describe the Arabic word for capitalism *ra's maliyah* as "a literal translation of our [Persian] word for capitalism" (117), and then they discuss Israel. Âl-e Ahmad states the problem not in terms of the existence of Israel on Palestinian land, but in terms of the activities of Israel as one of the hands of foreign capitalism, like Aramco and the other oil companies. He describes Nasser's behavior toward Israel as "demagoguery" (118), and asserts that the Arabs' real enemy is the oil companies rather than Israel. The officer, however, insists that "Israel must first be killed in the palaces of the Arab kings, and afterwards in Palestine itself" (119), that reactionary Arab leaders must be deposed, and Palestine liberated.   Later, Âl-e Ahmad reflects on their conversation, "thinking that the West has really used Israel as a cover for its own misdeeds, or as a way of hiding them. They have planted Israel in the heart of the Arab lands so that the Arabs would forget the real troublemakers in the midst of Israel's trouble-making, . . . the French and American capitalists." (120)

Âl-e Ahmad mentions Palestine again, when he describes a coffee vendor, "more of a beggar than a coffee-seller" (121) from Gaza. Âl-e Ahmad continues,

> Frankly, these Gaza Arabs who've fled Palestine are an embarrassment to Islam.   How many years since that happened? It must be 10 years now. These gentlemen have been installed in their tents as beggars with no responsibility, and they are the basis for the dispute between Israel and Egypt. They have no jobs, no homes, no way to return to Israel, and they aren't allowed to enter Egypt. (122)

Again, it is not so much the occupation of Palestine, but the the existence of the Palestinian refugees and the "dispute between Israel and Egypt" to which Âl-e Ahmad objects. In fairness to Âl-e Ahmad, however, his understanding of the Israeli/Palestinian issue changed significantly following the 1967 war, as we shall see.

Âl-e Ahmad's criticism of the Saudi government is such that he wants Mecca, Medina, 'Arafat and Mina internationalized, managed by a joint council of Islamic nations and removed from Saudi control, because "as it stands now the Hajj is mechanized barbarism" (123):

> I'm saying that every year a million people take part in these rites, and that if there were order, facilities, procedures, and creativity, there could be great power. After all, the Muslim people of today don't have to accept pre-Islamic Arab life or Arab ignorance in order to partake of such primitiveness!" (124)

Âl-e Ahmad accuses the Saudi government of caring more for itself than for the Islamic holy places and rites entrusted to it. Âl-e Ahmad describes Jedda:

> We passed Eve's grave at this point. High, thick walls, just like the walls of an old ice house, with a short, narrow door in one corner. It had fallen into disrepair and looked worse than the most obscure and forgotten shrine of an Imam's descendant in Abarqu. The grandmother of humanity! Then we passed the Foreign Ministry. Such splendor! Then the Bedouin bazaar, which was still bustling. Then we passed alongside "The Palace of the Great King," with its walls reaching to the sky and its gate guarded by soldiers shouldering machine guns. Then we passed beside a low, crumbling wall, which they had laid around a large tract of land. "The Place of Prayer." The place for Friday prayers. (125)

In Medina, in the Prophet's Mosque, he relates taking a cup of water distributed by a Berber woman:

> They sit in groups at the base of the mosque's columns with rectangular stainless steel trays full of empty cups large enough for one gulp. Grandiosely written in Arabic on the tray was "Endowment of the Ministry of Pilgrimage Affairs and Religious Trusts." In any case, supplied in lieu of the 10 or 20 electric water coolers which are in every government office, it too is another example of how Hajj affairs are organized, and of the Saudi government's attentiveness and concern for the condition of the hajjis. (126)

He complains as well, that the Saudis do not respect the customs of the Shi'i pilgrims who come on the Hajj. At the graveyard of Uhud,

> Two groups of Iranian hajjis sat on either side [of the common grave of the martyrs of the battle of Uhud], wailing mournfully with great excitement in the shur mode, in a way that would have melted the hardest heart, crying and beating themselves about the head and chest. Others, however, stood and prayed in the middle of the cemetery, and two or three young Arabs came to prohibit evil, saying "Forbidden! Forbidden! Do not make a mosque of the graves of your fathers," repeating the surah and rotating passionately. No one paid any attention, however. (127)

Especially hurtful to Âl-e Ahmad is the Saudis' not allowing the Shi'is to mark the graves of the four Shi'i Imams in the Baqi' Cemetery in Medina. When he visits the graveyard, where his brother had worked to put stone borders around the four graves and where he was now buried as well, he describes how all the grave markers have been smashed:

> the work of the Wahhabis of 40 years ago when they came to power in Saudi Arabia. Did they do all this simply out of Wahhabi prejudice? .... Or perhaps they wanted to keep other graves from standing out too prominently near the Prophet's grave? After all, the distance between the graveyard and the Prophet's Mosque is less than 200 meters. No. One cannot expect to find that much intelligence—especially back then—among these Saudis. Someone who knows these expressions and explanations will conclude in his mind that they ought to put up a monument in the middle of the graveyard instead of individual graves for all these great people, with all their names and the dates of their births carved on a stone. One must conclude that the Saudis aren't capable of managing these shrines. Medina and Mecca must be set free from the disgrace of these gentlemen and be declared two international Islamic cities. Suppose I'm stupid and you Saudis are extremely wise! What right have we to reduce to dust shrines which are a part of Muslim daily life? (128)

But again, it is Arab ignorance and primitivism on the part of the Saudi monarchy which Âl-e Ahmad criticizes, manifested in Saudi poor taste. He describes the Prophet's Mosque in Medina:

> They [the Saudi government] were totally negligent in the Prophet's Mosque. Architecturally it is half Andalusian, half Ottoman, with a veneer of cement slabs in three or four colors. They have laid huge slabs of red, cream, and black concrete alongside one another and stacked them to the top. Covering the roof were larger, continuous pieces, no doubt supported by iron rods embedded in the cement, instead of these beautiful black stones that surround Medina and which they could easily have shaped and laid over the building. I really wanted to know who the architect was so I could collar him and say, "Sir! The supernatural magnificence of a building like this must be expressed with the simplest natural materials. It must be achieved with stone, not these molded concrete slabs. You, who were responsible for the construction of such grandeur in Medina, did it not occur to you to seek assistance from engineers and architects from all Muslim countries? Or consultation on the various kinds of vaulted arches that were brought to Andalusia from India? (129)

Later, he describes Mecca in much the same fashion:

> It appears that even the Kaaba will have been rebuilt with steel reinforced concrete by next year, just like the Prophet's Mosque. They've already taken out one side of the old outer colonnade, the one facing the mas'a, and will undoubtedly destroy its other parts with a year or two. It's true that the space available for circumambulation will be wider and that a larger crowd—three or four times the size of the current one will be able to circumambulate the Kaaba, but the problem is that they will still be using these cement slabs attached to reinforced concrete pillars, and building upward with them. With beautiful hard rock close at hand, they still use this cement and these cement forms. From up here the Kaaba is just half the size I had imagined. That individual who was architect of this new outer colonnade was evidently unaware that when you destroy proportion you change architecture. The Kaaba is still the same size, but they've made the outer corridor twice as wide, and twice as high. How about destroying the Kaaba itself and making it higher and larger? Out of reinforced concrete, no doubt? (130)
> The streets have neon lighting, and there are multi-colored mini-skyscrapers along the streets, with garish colors in the new windows, such as bright green and burgundy. Very primitive, and it badly defaces the city. (131)
> Neon fills the streets everywhere. It's even on top of the House's minarets and the Kaaba itself. When it pleased God to

have a house built on the surface of this land, he should have realized that land would one day fall into the hands of the Saudi government, and that its doors and walls would be covered with neon because of the exigencies of oil exploration. I'm not advocating replacing neon with kerosene, but, for the sake of dignity, why shouldn't they order specially designed lamps from these companies that would be worthy of such grandeur, and not have even the house of God become a common consumer for Pennsylvania? (132)

Âl-e Ahmad even complains about the Islamic lunar calendar, as confining Islam to Saudi Arabia:

There will be, according to me, one day, and according to another person a two-day interval between the announcement by these Saudi gentlemen and the appearance of the new moon according to the Shi'i calendar. It's quite clear, however, that the 'Ayd must be observed according to the celestial position of this location. A guy who comes from Indonesia by way of Turkey will surely have a different lunar calendar, but the rites of the Hajj must be enacted here. I don't see why the Hajj couldn't be kept in one season of the year—in the solar calendar. Wasn't it this way originally, so the hajjis from northern countries wouldn't defer their journey to some year when 'Ayd-e Qorbân occurred during the winter? I realized that the Hajj, with this lunar calendar, has confined Islam to the equatorial regions. (133)

Later, though, he seems to contradict himself, deciding that the lunar calendar has indeed been used historically throughout the region; apparently as long as it was not used just by Arabs, it is acceptable:

Tonight I realized why the lunar calendar is the official one here instead of the solar calendar, throughout this region, from ancient Babylon to Egypt. The solar calendar can have no meaning in these parts. The winter here is like the fall, and both of them are like summer. They have had to rely on the moon to light the cold nights. For this reason religious rites are usually held during the first half of the month. Religious rites, celebrations, and days of mourning usually take place on days when the moon if full and high, or is on the rise, so the desert, with its cool nights, will be well-lit for religious ceremony. (134)

Âl-e Ahmad's feelings toward Arabic, however, are separate from his feelings towards Arabs. As in "The Pilgrimage," Arabic has value as the language of religion. He remarks, "This Arabic is certainly a good language for enjoining and prohibiting" (135), emphasizing its role in establishing a moral code. And Arabic, as the language of religion, has great power for him:

> I was feeling so good this morning that I said hello to everyone, didn't feel like a hypocrite when I prayed, nor that I was doing my ablutions out of imitation. Yesterday and the day before I still couldn't believe this was me performing a religious rite just like everyone else. I remember all the prayers and the short and long verses from the Quran I memorized as a child. Arabic words, however, weigh heavily on my mind and tongue, excessively so. I can't pronounce them quickly. In those days I could read them off like a litany with no problems. I realized this morning, however, that Arabic has become a heavy burden on my conscience. In the morning when I said "peace be upon you, O Prophet," I had a sudden start. I could see the Prophet's grave and the people circumambulating. They were climbing all over one another to kiss the shrine. The police were continually scrambling to prevent forbidden behavior. I started crying and abruptly fled the mosque. (136)

And he is impressed by Ali ibn Wa'il's son, of seven or eight, being "very glib. I would not have imagined that there could have been such a smooth-talking young Arabic speaker." (137)

However, as he does in "The Pilgrimage" and "Customs and Excise," Âl-e Ahmad makes a distinction between the Arabic of the Quran and spoken Arabic, especially when it is spoken by Arabs. This, in one sense, is a distinction between religious and secular Arabic, but in another sense, it is a distinction between Arabic and Arabs. He introduces the conversations he has with Arabs as a chance to practice his Arabic:

> When I left the mosque I went into a coffee house. . . so I could practice my Arabic. (138)
> I greeted a young man sitting in a corner, and we exchanged pleasantries. I asked him a few questions for Arabic practice. (139)
> I asked if this was the road to the Fath Mosque, also to practice my Arabic. (140)

Later, when he begins to feel cross, he doesn't speak to another Arab because he "didn't feel like practicing Arabic anymore." (141) One gets the impression that knowing Arabic is more important than knowing Arabs.

Yet Âl-e Ahmad says that his own Arabic is very poor. He refers to his "broken, halting Arabic," his "terrible Arabic." (142) And in fact it is more often the case that Âl-e Ahmad is misunderstood than the reverse. In the Airport Hajj Village, two Saudi Arabian boy scouts walk through with "two red-haired Europeans in shorts.... I asked the Saudi Arabian boys in my broken, halting Arabic, 'Are you sure these people are Muslims, that you bring them here?' They either didn't understand what I said or chose not to answer. The word 'Muslim', however, is intelligible to any deaf person from the mouth of any mute." (143)

According to Âl-e Ahmad, it is not just a case of his Arabic being terrible, but of the Arabs' stubborn refusal to understand it. Indeed, Âl-e Ahmad is quite put out when he is not understood. Later, visiting a library, he speaks to the director: "I told him I was an Iranian and a man of books. I asked him many questions, and he was at a loss. He was director of the library, but he couldn't understand broken Arabic." (144) Instead, he has to call his assistant, an Afghani from Kabul, with whom Âl-e Ahmad can converse.

The one place where Âl-e Ahmad was apparently easily understood was at a coffee house, where he orders eggs, bread, tea and mint: "He did understand my Arabic." (145) Otherwise, he declares, "It is impossible to talk to these Arabs. Try to say two words and you will get into a thousand difficulties. They don't understand most of your Arabic." (146)

Âl-e Ahmad understands the problem to be with Arab attitudes, not with his use of the Arabic language. On two different occasions, an Arab and an Iranian raise the subject of Âl-e Ahmad's moustache. Both times, he fends off their questions, and they leave in a bad temper. Yet he declares:

> Even that Iranian fellow who was wanting to know what sect I follow was simply looking for someone to talk to, to find a peer for a moment in the midst of the strangeness of this journey. This young Arab, however, was a resident of the shrine area, and he was just trying to show off his own superiority. Just like the French in the Parisian shrine areas, and their behavior towards foreigners, or just like the people of Mashhad. (147)

While being a resident of the shrine area may explain the Arab's behavior, Âl-e Ahmad's explanation of the Iranian's is still unconvincing. It is clear that his perception of both incidents has been colored by the nationality of the people involved.

But Arabic when it is spoken by non-Arabs is a common language that Muslims everywhere understand, and as such a powerful tool for Islamic unity. It is only the Arabs who make Arabic difficult for Âl-e Ahmad. He hears three Pakistanis preaching in Arabic, one who "spoke fluently and eloquently." (148) Another, "who looked like an Indian, [was] speaking in relatively clear Arabic.... And in such epic language. His upper teeth were pushed forward and his lips were parted; yet he spoke of faith, of Islam, and of the great danger to the Western world in the event of Islamic unity." (149)

Later, he sees another "non-Arab who preached in literary Arabic. I was strongly reminded of Sa'di." (150) Here Âl-e Ahmad has come full circle, dissociating Arabic from Arabs, and associating it with a great Persian poet and cultural hero.

At the end of *Lost in the Crowd*, Âl-e Ahmad asks himself why he has made the pilgrimage, and thinks of his brother, "who had come here to the seat of Wahhabi power to keep the remnants of Shi'ism alive" and died in Saudi Arabia. (151) Watching a woman with her child walking through the praying crowds toward the Kaaba, he realizes that

> the master of this House was that woman. Why had she come here, really, to so fearlessly move her womanly presence next to the Stone? I realized that it is worthwhile that the Kaaba has served for centuries and centuries as a refuge for every weary person, for this forsaken humanity, confounded by poverty, oppression, and anomie, like a wailing wall, if it answers even one of this woman's prayers. (152)

According to Manochehr Dorraj, Âl-e Ahmad "felt reborn while performing the ritual of pilgrimage. In Mecca he found a sense of peace, serenity, cohesion, and unity in life—a feeling of closeness to his fellow men he had never found before." (153) The reading in this work of *Lost in the Crowd* does not go so far. As discussed earlier, Âl-e Ahmad, in choosing to talk about his belief in Islam, qualified it. The conclusion of *Lost in the Crowd* is also qualified, more opaque than transparent. But in his presentation of the woman at the Kaaba and affirmation of its worth, Âl-e Ahmad admits to some kind of faith.

Dorraj also characterizes Âl-e Ahmad as a "protagonist of Islamic values, pro-Arab, and anti-Western." (154) It would be difficult to characterize the works discussed here as pro-Arab. Âl-e Ahmad affirms Shi'i Islam as essentially Iranian, but also as essentially non-Arab, and in the works discussed he presents the Arab Other as primitive, violent, ugly, and stupid. His position might be characterized as an uneasy compromise between Persian Iranian cultural nationalism, set against the Arab Other, and Islam set against Western imperialism as the Other, a position achievable only by de-Arabizing Islam.

However, Âl-e Ahmad's views changed significantly following the 1967 war, as can be seen in *Safar beh Valâyet-e Esrâ'il* [Journey to the State of Israel] (1984), the account of his trip to Israel in 1962 and response to the war in 1967. In the first part of the book, Âl-e Ahmad reveals his sympathy for the Jews and admiration for the achievements of Israel, particularly the assimilation of Jewish emigrants through Hebrew language education, and the kibbutz system. He admits that one of the reasons for his admiration is his anti-Arab feelings:

> I, the non-Arab Eastern man, . . . having been beaten so many times by this ignoble Arab, am happy at the presence of Israel in the East, the presence of Israel that can cut the oil pipelines of these sheikhs; that plants the seed of the demand for justice and right in the heart of any Bedouin Arab; and creates a nuisance for their lawless, outdated governments. (155)

The final chapter, however, "Âghâz-e Yek Nefrat" [The Beginning of a Hatred], was written in response to the 1967 war, and published as a separate article that same year. In that chapter, Âl-e Ahmad no longer sees Israel as a progressive, democratic country, independent of both East and West, but as an agent of Western imperialism. He condemns the Zionist occupation of Palestine and the plight of the Palestinian refugees, and refutes his previous views:

> If the conscience of the European intellectual is bothered by having agreed to that killing of the Jews, what does the Iranian intellectual say? That Esther was his queen and Mordechai the minster of his Achaemenid king, and Daniel the Prophet is his prophet. The conscience of the Iranian intellectual should be bothered by the fact that Iranian oil burns in the tanks and airplanes that are killing his Arab and Muslim brothers. (156)

Here, Âl-e Ahmad has moved beyond his earlier position. The Other is no longer the Arab, but Western imperialism, and Iranian cultural nationalism is placed within the Islamic response to the West.

Throughout his works, Âl-e Ahmad had unfailingly struggled to maintain what he saw as Iranian cultural authenticity. (157) By the time of his death, according to Roy Mottahedeh, this struggle had turned to grief for a threatened cultural heritage. (158)

Although he holds anti-Arab views, Âl-e Ahmad's response to the issue of Iranianness moves him away from the men and closer to the women earlier discussed. Like Saffârzâdeh and Dâneshvar, Âl-e Ahmad affirms Shi'i Islam as an essential part of Iranianness. Âl-e Ahmad sets Islam against Western imperialism and materialism, in defense of Persian Iranian culture and of humanity. Unable to believe in Westernizing modernization or Marxism, Âl-e Ahmad perhaps had nowhere else to go but to Islam, to return to his own roots as it were, and then to decide that they were in fact authentic Iranian roots as well.

Notes

1. Michael Craig Hillmann, "Introduction," *By the Pen*, by Jalâl Âl-e Ahmad, translated by M. R. Ghanoonparvar (Austin, TX: The University of Texas at Austin Center for Middle Eastern Studies, Middle East Monographs No. 8, 1988), p. ix.

2. Michael Craig Hillmann, "The Modernist Trend in Persian Literature and Its Social Impact," *Iranian Studies* 15 (1982): 17. His own footnote (5) reads: "Jalâl Âl-e Ahmad, *Kârnâmeh-ye Seh Sâleh* (Tehrân: Ketâb-e Zamân, 1967), p. 164, cites religion, language, and literature as cultural factors determining his personality as an Iranian. Idem, *Khasi dar Miqât* (Tehrân: Nil, 1966), pp. 105-106, sees cultural identity as determined by language, culture and tradition(s)."

3. Jalâl Âl-e Ahmad, *Gharbzadegi* [Plagued by the West], second printing (Tehrân: Âgâh, 1964); translated by Paul Sprachman (Delmar, NY: Caravan Books, 1982), p. 37.

4. Hillmann, "The Modernist Trend in Persian Literature," p. 17.

5. Reza Barâheni, *The Crowned Cannibals: Writings on Repression in Iran* (New York: Vintage Books, 1977), pp. 11-12.

6. Jalâl Âl-e Ahmad, "Samad va Afsâneh-ye 'Avâm" [Samad and the Folk Legend], Ârash No. 18 (November/December 1968): 5-12; translated by Leonardo P. Alishan, *Iranian Society: An Anthology of Writings by Jalâl Âl-e Ahmad*, compiled and edited by Michael Craig Hillmann (Costa Mesa, CA: Mazdâ, 1982),.pp. 134-142.

7. Michael Craig Hillmann, "Introduction," Lost in the Crowd, by Jalâl Âl-e Ahmad, translated by John Green (Washington, DC: Three Continents Press, 1985), p. xxix.

8. Âl-e Ahmad deals with the same cultural contradictions, on a more personal level, in *Sangi bar Guri* [A Stone on a Grave] (Tehrân: Ravâq, 1981).

9. Michael Craig Hillmann, "Iranian Nationalism and Modernist Persian Literature," *Essays on Nationalism and Asian Literatures*, edited by Michael Craig Hillmann. *Literature East and West* 23 (1987): 74.

10. Jalâl Âl-e Ahmad, Jalâl, "Gonâh" [The Sin], *Seh'târ*, third printing (Tehrân: Amir Kabir, 1970), pp. 81-90; translated by Raymond Cowart, *Iranian Society*, pp. 63-69.

11. Jalâl Âl-e Ahmad, "Seh'târ," *Seh'târ*, third printing (Tehrân: Amir Kabir, 1970), pp. 9-16; translated by Terence Odlin, *Iranian Society*, pp. 58-62.

12. Jalâl Âl-e Ahmad, "Eftâr-e Bimowqe'" [The Untimely Breaking of the Fast], *Did o Bâzdid* [Exchange of Visits], fifth printing (Tehrân: Amir Kabir, 1970), pp. 55-70; translated by Carter Bryant, *Iranian Society*, pp. 48-57.

13. Jalâl Âl-e Ahmad, "Ziyârat" [The Pilgrimage], *Did o Bâzdid* [Exchange of Visits], fifth printing (Tehrân: Amir Kabir, 1970), pp. 37-54; translated by Henry D. G. Law, *Iranian Society*, pp. 34-42.

14. Hillmann, "Introduction," *Lost in the Crowd*, p. xxxi.

15. Jalâl Âl-e Ahmad, "Al-Gomârak va al-Makus" [Customs and Excise], in *Seh'târ*, third printing (Tehran: Amir Kabir, 1970), pp. 177-200. My translation draws heavily upon an unpublished translation by A. Reza Navabpour and Robert Wells, in the possession of Michael Hillmann.

16. Hillmann, "Introduction," *Lost in the Crowd*, p. xxxi.

17. Âl-e Ahmad, *Plagued by the West*, pp. 11-12.

18. Ibid., p. 108.

19. Ibid.

20. Ibid., p. 15.

21. Ibid., p. 16.

22. Ibid.

23. Ibid., p. 17.

24. Ibid., p. 16.

25. Ibid., p. 29.

26. Ibid., p. 111.

27. Jalâl Âl-e Ahmad, *Khasi dar Miqât* [Lost in the Crowd] (Tehrân: Nil, 1966); translated by John Green (Washington, DC: Three Continents Press, 1985), p. 123.

28. Hillmann, "Introduction," *Lost in the Crowd*, p. xxxi.

29. Michael Craig Hillmann, "Preface," *Iranian Society*, p. xi.

30. Âl-e Ahmad, *Lost in the Crowd*, p. 123.

31. Ibid., p. 6.

32. Ibid., pp. 57-58.

33. Âl-e Ahmad, *Plagued by the West*, p. 48.

34. Hillmann, "Introduction," *Lost in the Crowd*, p. xxx.

35. Âl-e Ahmad, *Lost in the Crowd*, pp. 61-63.

36. Ibid., p. 114.

37. Ibid., p. 44.
38. Âl-e Ahmad, *Plagued by the West*, p. 51.
39. Hillmann, "Introduction," *Lost in the Crowd*, p. xxxi.
40. Âl-e Ahmad, *Lost in the Crowd*, p. 49.
41. Ibid., p. 10.
42. Ibid., p. 11.
43. Ibid., p. 55.
44. Ibid., p. 22.
45. Ibid., p. 12.
46. Ibid., p. 16.
47. Ibid., pp. 16-17.
48. Ibid., p. 19.
49. Ibid., p. 55.
50. Ibid., pp. 27, 44-45.
51. Ibid., pp. 53-54.
52. Ibid., p. 19.
53. Ibid., p. 40.
54. Ibid., p. 26.
55. Ibid., p. 72.
56. Ibid., p. 38.
57. Ibid., p. 62.
58. Ibid., p. 69.
59. Ibid., pp. 96-97.
60. Ibid., p. 118.
61. Ibid.
62. Ibid., p. 33.
63. *The Cambridge Encyclopedia of the Middle East and North Africa*, edited by Trevor Mostyn and Albert Hourani (Cambridge: Cambridge University Press, 1988), s.v. "Culture: Islam," by Ian K. A. Howard, pp. 160-177.
64. Âl-e Ahmad, *Lost in the Crowd*, p. 46.
65. Ibid., pp. 92-93.
66. Ibid., p. 13.
67. Ibid., pp. 13-14.
68. Ibid., p. 82.
69. Ibid., p. 106.
70. Ibid., p. 36.
71. Ibid., p. 37.
72. Ibid., p. 51.
73. Ibid., p. 106.
74. Ibid., p. 33.
75. Ibid., p. 7.
76. Ibid.
77. Ibid., p. 50.
78. Ibid., p. 16.
79. Ibid., p. 120.
80. Ibid., p. 31.

81. Ibid., p. 8.
82. Ibid., p. 11.
83. Ibid., p. 8.
84. Ibid., p. 13.
85. Ibid., p. 71.
86. Ibid., p. 93.
87. Ibid., p. 31.
88. Ibid., pp. 30-31.
89. Ibid., p. 32.
90. Ibid., p. 106.
91. Ibid.
92. Ibid., p. 107.
93. Ibid., p. 50.
94. Ibid., p. 38.
95. Ibid., p. 83.
96. Ibid., p. 38.
97. Ibid., p. 23.
98. Ibid., p. 29.
99. Ibid., p. 30.
100. Ibid., p. 41.
101. Âl-e Ahmad, *Plagued by the West*, p. 56.
102. Hillmann, "Introduction," *Lost in the Crowd*, p. xxxi.
103. Âl-e Ahmad, *Lost in the Crowd*, p. 14.
104. Ibid., p. 30.
105. Ibid., p. 82.
106. Ibid., p. 93.
107. Ibid., p. 91.
108. Ibid., p. 55.
109. Ibid., p. 114.
110. Ibid., p. 45.
111. Ibid., p. 118.
112. Ibid., p. 29.
113 Ibid., p. 69.
114. Ibid., p. 32.
115. Ibid., p. 9.
116. Ibid., p. 72.
117. Ibid.
118. Ibid.
119. Ibid., p. 73.
120. Ibid.
121. Ibid., p. 16.
122. Ibid.
123. Ibid., pp. 31, 91.
124. Ibid., p. 85.
125. Ibid., p. 10.
126. Ibid., p. 40.
127. Ibid., p. 30.

128. Ibid., pp. 28-29.
129. Ibid., p. 40.
130. Ibid., pp. 58-59.
131. Ibid., p. 60
132. Ibid., pp. 60-61.
133. Ibid., p. 21.
134. Ibid., p. 97.
135. Ibid., p. 94.
136. Ibid., pp. 21-22.
137. Ibid., p. 54.
138. Ibid., p. 17.
139. Ibid., p. 25.
140. Ibid., p. 49.
141. Ibid., p. 50.
142. Ibid., p. 9.
143. Ibid., p. 9.
144. Ibid., p. 52.
145. Ibid., p. 37.
146. Ibid., p. 50.
147. Ibid.
148. Ibid., p. 18.
149. Ibid.
150. Ibid., p. 55.
151. Ibid., p. 115.
152. Ibid.
153. Manochehr Dorraj, *From Zarathustra to Khomeini: Populism and Dissent in Iran* (Boulder, CO: Lynne Rienner, 1990), p. 111.
154. Ibid.
155. Jalâl Âl-e Ahmad, *Safar beh Valâyet-e Esrâ'il* [Journey to the State of Israel] (Tehrân: Ravâq, 1984), pp. 59-62; translation mine.
156. Ibid., pp. 91-92.
157. Hillmann, "Iranian Nationalism and Modernist Persian Literature," p. 73.
158. Roy Mottahedeh, *The Mantle of the Prophet: Religion and Politics in Iran* (New York: Pantheon Books, 1985), p. 323.

Chapter 5

Conclusion

As we have seen, Iranianness has been an important theme in modern Persian literature from its very beginnings. As part of the answer to the question of self-definition, some Persian Iranian writers, like Mohammad Ali Jamâlzâdeh, Sâdeq Hedâyat, Sâdeq Chubak, Mehdi Akhavân-e Sâles, and Nâder Nâderpour, have used images of Arabs to define an Iran as a nation and themselves as Iranian in contrast to an Arab Other. The Arab Other is a reverse definition of the Iranian Self, for some in terms of race or language, for others in terms of religion, history and culture as well. Moreover, the Arab Other is a metaphor which may also represent the Islamic, or Western Other, or certain aspects of Iranian life which the writer would not be able to criticize openly, for example, the monarchy.

However, defining Iranianness is not only a literary concern, but is essential to the creation of an "Iranian" national identity in the 20th century. Indeed, the development of Iranian nationalism in the 19th and 20th centuries, in literary and political discourse, may be seen as the "ideological creation of the nation" suggested by Benedict Anderson. According to Anderson, one cannot 'define' a nation by a set of external and abstract criteria, or objective social facts. Instead the nation is 'an imagined political community', something which is 'thought out', 'created'. (1) Thus, literary works are both a reflection of and, more importantly, a part of an ideological discourse, part of the creation of modern Iranian nationalism and Iran as a modern nation.

Iranian nationalist discourse set for itself the task of defining Iran as a nation and formulating an Iranian nationalism. One way to define the Iranian Self is by defining the Other—Western, Islamic, Arab—in terms of language, race, history, culture, religion or ideology. (2) Thus, Shâhrokh Meskoob sets the Iranian Self against an Arab Other, defining Iranianness in terms of Persian language and pre-Islamic history. Manochehr Dorraj, however, sees Shi'i Islam as an essential part of Iranianness, and sets the Iranian Self against the Western (non-Islamic) Other. The terms of these definitions, however, are set by two very different understandings of nationalism.

Leon Poliakov describes the Western paradigm of nationalism, based on the myths of a common origin, the linguistic evidence of which became proof of race, and of a Golden Age, to which the nation might return by returning to its original cultural, linguistic and racial purity (all terms being interchangeable). Indeed, Western nationalist and racist ideas, particularly the existence of an "Aryan" and "Semitic" race, developed hand-in-hand. Indeed, the central motif of racism is "purity," the same purity which informs the Western national model and so precludes a multi-ethnic nationalism. Meskoob defines Iranianness in terms of this Western nationalist discourse. It is this same understanding of nationalism which was largely propagated by the Pahlavi government.

However, Dorraj defines Iranianness in terms of the "alternative Islamic ideology" which emerged in the 1960s and 1970s in Iran. (3) In what one might call an Islamist rather than a nationalist view, the Other is seen in ideological terms, and it is this view which is reflected in the Islamic Republic.

The same definitions of Iranianness, in terms of the Iranian Self and of the Arab or Western Other, and the same formulations of Iranian nationalism appear in literary discourse.

In Mohammad Ali Jamâlzâdeh's "Persian is Sugar," Persian and Iranian are synonymous, as are Arab (or French or Âzarbâyjâni) and foreign. While Jamâlzâdeh regards Islam as integral to an Iranian national identity, he objects to a backward Islam, and to Arabness as foreign. Jamâlzâdeh associates an Arab Other with religious superstition and backwardness, and defines the Iranian Self as Persian and Muslim. Yet, while Jamâlzâdeh uses the Western national model, seeing Iranian nationalism in terms of a common language and identity, he does not support Western racism.

Sâdeq Hedâyat loathes the Arab Other, and abhors Islam as an Arab religion. In "Seeking Absolution" and *Parvin the Sâsânid Girl*, he portrays Arabs as dark-skinned, dirty, diseased, ugly, stupid, cruel and shameless, bestial and demonic. Moreover, Hedâyat portrays present-day Iranian Muslims as corrupt and hypocritical. Only his Sâsânid Iranians are attractive, courageous, intelligent, cultured and virtuous. Hedâyat idealizes the pre-Islamic, Zoroastrian past as the Golden Age of Iran. In his view, Iran's true cultural identity, shared with "Aryan" India, was destroyed by the Arab Muslim invaders, who replaced Iran's superior civilization with the brutal and bloodthirsty culture and religion of their own. Hedâyat, often admired as a writer of sensitivity and progressive human values, espouses Western racism and anti-Semitism. He believes that "Aryan" Iranians are racially superior to the "Semitic" Arabs.

Sâdeq Chubak's view differs only somewhat from that of Hedâyat. In *The Patient Stone*, Iranian rootlessness and alienation are the result of history: the Arab Muslims destroyed a great Iranian civilization and could not replace it. Iranians, both individually and socially, have consequently suffered because they were cut off from their own, true Iranian history, art, and culture. Chubak's characters also reveal racist thinking, and a level of anti-Arab sentiment throughout *The Patient Stone*. Chubak portrays the Arab (and Indian) Other as hypocritical, ugly and cruel, while the Iranian Self has been defeated and further corrupted by Semitic hypocrisy in the form of Islam, for Chubak sees the institution of Shi'i Islam in Iran only as a tool for oppression. At the same time, he rejects Iranian chauvinism. Zoroastrianism and the history of Iranian kings hold no answers either. Indeed, Chubak goes so far as to equate Zoroastrianism with Islam, and to reject both. However, he rejects Islam on two levels: because it is a religion, which in Chubak's view offers no answers, and because it is an Arab religion. For Chubak, there are no answers; life is indeed without meaning. However, alienation and existential despair are both universal, and historically and culturally specific. Existential despair informs the Self more than categories of Iranianness or Arabness, yet Chubak maintains those categories as well. While Chubak rejects Aryanism, his writings do support anti-Semitism.

Mehdi Akhavân-e Sâles, like Hedâyat, blames the Muslim Arab invaders for destroying Iran's true cultural identity and longs for a return to pre-Islamic Zoroastrian culture and greatness. According to "The Ending of the *Shâhnâmeh*," the ending of Zoroastrian Iranian culture with the defeat of the Sâsânid empire and the coming of Islam has resulted in ruin and despair, which can be resolved only by returning to Iran's pre-Islamic golden age. The Iranian Self was pure, bright and beautiful, but has been corrupted by the Arab Other, false, dark, and evil. Akhavân decries "Semitic *and* Arabic *and* Islamic" influence on the "heritage of our own Aryan ancestors." In so doing he echoes

Hedâyat's view of Iranians and Arabs as two different and unequal races, one Aryan and superior, the other Semitic and inferior.

Nâder Nâderpour rejects Arabs and Islam as alien, and fundamentally opposed to true Iranian culture and values. "Here and There" repeats the same image of Arabs as found in Hedâyat and Akhavân, as savage, alien intruders who have destroyed a superior Iranian civilization. Nâderpour portrays the Arab Other as dark, savage and inhuman, in images of the irrational, blood and the moon; he portrays the Iranian Self as the creator of an enlightened civilization, in images of Zoroastrian fire, the sun and springtime. Nâderpour sees Islam not so much as wrong in itself, but wrong because it is Arab, and therefore backward and cruel. In "Here and There," Nâderpour compares the establishment of the Islamic Republic to the Arab Muslim conquest of the Sâsânid empire, and suggests that it is in fact a continuation of that same defeat of superior Iranian culture at the hands of ignorant and intolerant Arabs. In Nâderpour's view, to be a devout Muslim, or a supporter of the Islamic Republic of Iran, is to be Arab and therefore not Iranian, indeed therefore almost less than human. Like Hedâyat, Chubak and Akhavân, his is an anti-Islamic and anti-Arab view.

All of the men put Iranian nationalism in terms of the Western nationalist paradigm, with its myth of common origin and subsequent insistence on linguistic homogeneity, from which follows an insistence on racial homogeneity, and all but Jamâlzâdeh, a cleric's son, espouse Western anti-Semitism as well. All of them set the Iranian Self against the Arab Other, and for all but Jamâlzâdeh again, the Arab Other is also the Islamic Other. The women's writings, however, reflect a very different approach to nationalism.

Forugh Farrokhzâd was not concerned in her poetry with the question of Arabs and Iranians. On some level at least these are issues of masculine history and politics, from which Farrokhzâd, as a woman, had been excluded and at the same time to which she attached little importance. Unlike the men, she has no need to establish an historical identity as an Iranian, nor does she need to establish her cultural identity as an Iranian at the expense of another. There are no Arabs or Iranians as such in her poems, only individuals. Like Hedâyat, Chubak and Nâderpour, Farrokhzâd did not believe in Islam, and criticizes the institution of Islam in "The Windup Doll" and "I Feel Sorry for the Garden," but, unlike Hedâyat or Chubak, she criticizes it as an Iranian, not as an alien or Arab institution. In "I Feel Sorry for the Garden," she is equally critical of religion, the mother's fault, and nationalism, the father's fault. At the same time, Farrokhzâd uses Islamic imagery in a very positive sense, as in "Someone Who Is Not Like Anyone," albeit from the perspective of a third-grade girl in South Tehrân.

Unlike the previous writers, she refuses to participate in the nationalist discourse. Perhaps that is why Farrokhzâd's anti-Islamic sentiments are not anti-Arab.

For Tâhereh Saffârzâdeh, as a practicing Muslim, Islam is a universal, not an Arab, phenomenon. She writes as Muslim first, and as an Iranian second. Her world view is not nationalist, but Islamic and universalist. Her Iranianness, in terms of geography, language, culture and history, provide the specific context within which she practices her Islam. Moreover, in poems about Iran, "The Stooping Ones" and "The Love Journey," Saffârzâdeh's vision of Iranianness includes Persian Iranian elements, other Iranian elements, and Islamic elements. In acknowledging a multi-ethnic Iran, Saffârzâdeh's Persian Iranianness is but one of many varieties. Saffârzâdeh portrays no Arab Other. Arab characters appear in her poems, not as Arabs but as another oppressed people, in "Through the Passageway of Silence and Torture," or as brothers in Islam, in "Homesickness." Most significant, however, is Saffârzâdeh's view of history, which essentially differs from that of Hedâyat, Chubak, Akhavân or Nâderpour. "Salmân's Journey" portrays the Arab Muslim invaders of Sâsânid Iran not as Arabs conquering Iran, but as Muslims bringing the liberating truth of Islam to a people waiting to accept it. Saffârzâdeh portrays Salmân as the exemplar of all Persian Muslims, just as Balâl represents the Africans and Suhaib the Europeans, all Companions of the Arab Prophet Mohammad. Their nationality is important only insofar as it underlines the internationalist character of Islam. Instead of a national or racial confrontation between Iranians and Arabs, Saffârzâdeh sees an ideological confrontation with Western imperialism and materialism, with anti-Islamic ideology. Hers is an Islamic political model, instead of the Western, and so very different, in the absence of Western nationalist and racist ideas, from that of the men previously discussed.

Simin Dâneshvar's treatment of Arabs is part of her very different definition of Iranianness. Dâneshvar allows for much difference among Iranians, but sees an essential unity at the level of myth and religion, where pre-Islamic Iranian mythology joins with Islam to produce a cultural synthesis which is essentially Iranian. While Jamâlzâdeh alone among the male authors treated above accepts Islam, he still sets an Iranian Self against an Arab Other. For Dâneshvar, however, Arab and Islamic elements in Iranian culture have an Iranian, rather than a foreign character. In *Savushun* she very nicely turns around Jamâlzâdeh's "Persian is as Sweet as Sugar," when what appears to be a villainous Arab turns out to be an unscrupulous Persian clergyman, and again in "Traitor's Intrigue," where the character of the Âqâ is both specifically Iranian and more generally, as a Muslim, universalist, and where Arabic is not a foreign language to Muslim Iranians. Like Saffârzâdeh, Dâneshvar also accepts ethnic diversity, unlike the male writers previously discussed. For Dâneshvar, there are Persian, Turkish, and Arab Iranians, but there is no Arab Other. In *Savushun*, Dâneshvar recognizes Arabs simply as Arabs. For Dâneshvar, like Saffârzâdeh, in "Traitors' Intrigue" and *Savushun* the Other is Western imperialism, manifested in Iran as the Pahlavi regime. Dâneshvar's view is very different from the Western nationalist and essentially racist view of the men.

Unlike Jamâlzâdeh, Hedâyat, Chubak, Akhavân-e Sâles, Nâderpour, and Âl-e Ahmad, the women do not reflect Western nationalist or racist ideas. They never use the terms "Aryan" or "Semite." They also accept ethnic diversity, while for the men, "Iranian" means "Persian." (Of course there are many male writers who do accept Iranian ethnic diversity, such as Samad Behrangi, Rezâ Barâheni, or Gholamhosayn Sâ'edi). Curiously, nationalism seems very much a masculine concern, perhaps because Iranian history and politics have been such a masculine affair. Yet, to pose the question in those terms suggests that Western nationalism is indeed a patriarchal construct. Hedâyat's accusations of sexual violation, Chubak's images of miscegenation, and Âl-e Ahmad's attention to the sexuality of Arabs and beauty (or lack thereof) of Arab women, and his defining Arab men as Arabs (whose province is nationality), but Arab women as women (whose province is sex), are all in line with that central motif of Western nationalism, "purity." Racial purity is encoded in sexual purity, which is possessed by women and enforced by men, and "miscegenation" is a violation of both.

Jalâl Âl-e Ahmad was truly caught between the views of the men and the women previously discussed, wanting both Iranian nationalism and Islam. However, Âl-e Ahmad moves away from the Western formulation of Iranian nationalism, towards Islam, and his attitudes toward Arabs change as well.

While Hedâyat, Akhavân-e Sâles and Nâderpour argue for an Iranianness based on a pre-Islamic "Aryan" cultural identity, and, along with Chubak, reject Islam and the Arabs as an alien "Semitic" presence, Âl-e Ahmad initially rejects Arabs but accepts Shi'i Islam as an integral part of Iranianness, along with Persian language and Persian Iranian culture. Like Jamâlzâdeh, Âl-e Ahmad recognizes Shi'i Islam as the world view of most Iranians. While he condemns superstition and rigid legalism, he values religious morality, Âl-e Ahmad also recognizes the potential Islam holds as a social and political force in Iran and the world, particularly the developing countries. Âl-e Ahmad also values Arabic as the language of revelation and religion, in "The Pilgrimage" and *Lost in the Crowd.* Moreover, Arabic is a language common to Muslims everywhere, and as such a powerful tool for Islamic unity. Furthermore, Âl-e Ahmad does not accept the ideology of Aryanism, or the view of history to which it gave rise. In *Plagued by the West,* Âl-e Ahmad refuses to glorify the Sâsânid empire as Iran's Golden Age. Instead, he presents Islam as being essentially not Arab but Iranian from its beginnings, depending upon an Iranian, Salmân the Persian, for its initial development, and reaching back even earlier to share the ideals of Mazdak and Mâni. According to Âl-e Ahmad, true Islam emerged only when it reached the Persian empire.

Âl-e Ahmad's desire to Iranicize and de-Arabize Islam, however, is motivated as much by his disliking things Arab as by his liking things Iranian. "Customs and Excise" and *Lost in the Crowd* reflect Âl-e Ahmad's view of the Arab Other as alien, primitive, stupid, greedy, deceitful, violent, ill-mannered and dirty. Âl-e Ahmad's position might be characterized as a difficult compromise between Persian Iranian cultural nationalism, set against the Arab Other, and Islam set against Western imperialism as the Other, a position he could maintain only by de-Arabizing Islam.

However, Âl-e Ahmad's views changed in response to the 1967 war. While he begrudgingly admires Israel's progress, in "The Beginning of a Hatred" he portrays Israel as an agent of Western imperialism, condemns the Zionist occupation of Palestine, and refutes his earlier anti-Arab views. The Arab is no longer the Other, only Western imperialism, and it is the larger Islamic Self which he defends against the West.

Âl-e Ahmad's answer to the question of Iranian nationalism moves him closer to Saffârzâdeh and Dâneshvar. Âl-e Ahmad affirms Shi'i Islam as an essential part of Iranianness, and sets Islam against Western imperialism and materialism, in defense of Iranian culture and of humanity.

The Iranian nationalist discourse, literary and political, set for itself the task of defining Iran as a nation and formulating an Iranian nationalism. But another problem arises with the Iranian adoption of Western nationalism. According to Partha Chatterjee,

> Nationalism sought to demonstrate the falsity of the colonial claim that the backward peoples were culturally incapable of ruling themselves in the conditions of the modern world. Nationalism denied the alleged inferiority of the colonized people; it also asserted that a backward nation could 'modernize' itself while retaining its cultural identity. It thus produced a discourse in which, even as it challenged the colonial claim to political domination, it also accepted the

very intellectual premises of 'modernity' on which colonial domination was based. (4)

There is a contradiction inherent in Iranian nationalism, which developed as a reaction to Western imperialism but used Western ideas to define Iranianness.

This contradiction was perhaps resolved, at least in nationalist thinking, by the choice of the Other. For some Iranian nationalists, the Other has been not so much the West, but the Arabs and Islam. Identifying Iran with the West, as fellow "Aryan" nations, allowed for the acceptance of Western modernization and the importation of Western culture, which was not perceived as a threat to Iranianness because it was not a culture of the Other but, on some level, of the Self. The myth of the common origin of Iranians, "proved" by categories of race ("Aryan") and language (Indo-European), and the myth of the pre-Islamic Golden Age, allowed Iran to fit the Western national model; and no matter if loyalty to that language and those cultural elements had to be encouraged, or enforced, among certain sections of the population.

In the 1960s and 1970s, however, an alternative Islamic ideology emerged, the result of "a deliberate effort on the part of Shari'ati and his cothinkers to politicize Islam and to present an alternative Islamic ideology to combat the hegemony of Western-inspired secular ideologies in political life." (5) And instead of trying to resolve anew the contradiction inherent in Iranian participation in the Western nationalist discourse, the alternative Islamic ideology rejected that discourse altogether. At the same time, this ideology is truly Iranian. According to Dorraj,

> The Iranian Revolution of 1979 must be understood not as a call for change but, as both Arendt and Benjamin have suggested, as an act of restoration—a halt to the rapid pace of development, and a revival of traditional cultural symbols.
> The revolution, its symbols, and its leaders emerged from the very depth of Iranian society. They were embedded in sacred political traditions and sanctioned cultural norms. The ulama represent a part of non-Western Iranian identity—what may be called "genuinely Iranian," insofar as Shi'ism has been the main source of cultural identification for the overwhelming majority since 1722. (6)

The irony of the Iranian nationalism of the Constitutional period (like that of many other countries) is that it emerged as a reaction to Western imperialism, but used Western ideas, of language, culture and common origin (history or race, and in fact all of the categories become interchangeable) to define Iranianness. What is significant about Iran's Islamic revolution is that it attempts to reject not only Western political, economic and cultural hegemony, but Western ideological hegemony as well. The establishment of the Islamic Republic of Iran is in itself a repudiation of the views of Hedâyat, Chubak, Akhavân and Nâderpour, in answer to the question of Islam and Iranianness.

Poliakov points out that "the Aryan theory does indeed belong to the tradition of anti-clericalism and anti-obscurantism" (7) as "scientific" nationalist and racist ideas developed to replace Christian theology. According to Poliakov,

> The tendency embodied in the ruling dynasty to claim a distinct and superior descent always clashed with the myth of Adam as a universal father—a myth which, according to a rabbinical apologist, was intended to teach all men that they are in reality equal.
>
> The Judaeo-Christian tradition was both anti-racist and anti-nationalist, and the social structure and barriers of the Middle Ages, with its feudal, horizontal hierarchies, no doubt helped the Church to translate this ideal into reality. If all men were equal before God, vertical and geographical distinctions should make no difference to the value of human beings. (8)

Thus, the Iranian experience parallels the European experience, where the Church (in theory) stands against nationalism and racism. The Islamic political model, the Islamic Caliphate, also (in theory) stands against nationalism and racism. The Islamic political model, the Islamic Caliphate, does not fit the Western model of political nationalism. But the Caliphate model, with its members' primary loyalty to the Muslim *ummah*, at the same time admits a multi-ethnic, cultural nationalism. And given Iran's multi-ethnic character, there may be no practical alternative but to appeal to Islam as a basis for national unity.

Âl-e Ahmad concludes *Plagued by the West*, by purifying his pen with a verse from the Quran. Let us end this work in the same way, but let us choose a different verse:

> O people! We have created you male and female, and have made you nations and tribes that ye may know one another. The noblest of you, in the sight of Allah, is the most righteous. Allah is Knower, Aware. (49:13)

Notes

1. Benedict Anderson, *Imagined Communities: Reflections on the Origin and Spread of Nationalism* (London: Verso, 1983); cited by Partha Chatterjee, *Nationalist Thought and the Colonial World: A Derivative Discourse* (London: Zed, 1986), pp. 19, 21.

2. See M. R. Ghanoonparvar, *In a Persian Mirror: Images of the West and Westerners in Iranian Fiction* (Austin: University of Texas Press, 1993).

3. Manochehr Dorraj, *From Zarathustra to Khomeini: Populism and Dissent in Iran* (Boulder, CO: Lynne Rienner, 1990), p. 111.

4. Chatterjee, *Nationalist Thought and the Colonial World*, p. 30.

5. Dorraj, *From Zarathustra to Khomeini*, p. 111.

6. Ibid., pp. vii-viii.

7. Leon Poliakov, *The Aryan Myth: A History of Racist and Nationalist Ideas in Europe*, translated by Edmund Howard (New York: Meridian, 1977), p. 328.

8. Ibid., p. 326.

Index